Educating for Peace and Human Rights

Educating for Peace and Human Rights

An Introduction

**Maria Hantzopoulos
and Monisha Bajaj**

BLOOMSBURY ACADEMIC
LONDON · NEW YORK · OXFORD · NEW DELHI · SYDNEY

BLOOMSBURY ACADEMIC
Bloomsbury Publishing Plc
50 Bedford Square, London, WC1B 3DP, UK
1385 Broadway, New York, NY 10018, USA
29 Earlsfort Terrace, Dublin 2, Ireland

BLOOMSBURY, BLOOMSBURY ACADEMIC and the Diana logo are trademarks
of Bloomsbury Publishing Plc

First published in Great Britain 2021

Cover design by Charlotte James
Cover image © ImageZoo / Alamy Stock Photo

A catalogue record for this book is available from the British Library.

Library of Congress Cataloging-in-Publication Data
Names: Hantzopoulos, Maria, author. | Bajaj, Monisha, author.
Title: Educating for peace and human rights: an introduction /
Maria Hantzopoulos and Monisha Bajaj.
Description: London; New York: Bloomsbury Academic, 2021. |
Includes bibliographical references and index.
Identifiers: LCCN 2020047679 | ISBN 9781350129726 (hardback) |
ISBN 9781350129733 (epub)
Subjects: LCSH: Peace–Study and teaching. | Human rights–Study and teaching.
Classification: LCC JZ5534 .H365 2021 | DDC 303.6/6071–dc23
LC record available at https://lccn.loc.gov/2020047679

ISBN: HB: 978-1-3501-2972-6
PB: 978-1-3501-2971-9
ePDF: 978-1-3501-2973-3
eBook: 978-1-3501-2974-0

Typeset by Deanta Global Publishing Services, Chennai, India
Printed and bound in Great Britain

To find out more about our authors and books visit www.bloomsbury.com and
sign up for our newsletters.

Contents

List of Illustrations vi
Acknowledgments vii
Copyright and Note on the Text ix
List of Abbreviations x

Introduction 1

1 Peace Education: The Foundations and Future Directions of a Field 15

2 Peace Education in Practice: Examples from the United States 35

3 Human Rights Education: Foundations, Frameworks, and Future Directions 51

4 Human Rights Education in Practice: Examples from South Asia 79

5 Bridging the Fields: Conceptualizing Dignity and Transformative Agency in Peace and Human Rights Education 95

6 Concluding Thoughts and the Way Ahead 115

Appendix: Annotated List of Further Reading in Peace and Human Rights Education 127
Notes 152
References 155
Index 176

Illustrations

Figures

0.1 CREDD Problem Tree 4

0.2 Envisioning a Culture of Peace, Justice, and Human
Rights Possibility Tree 8

1.1 Peace Education and Related Fields 26

3.1 Participatory Dimensions of Transformative Human Rights
Education 61

5.1 Educating for Peace and Human Rights Possibility Tree 97

5.2 Shared Tenets of Liberatory Education 98

5.3 Core Components of Transformative Agency 112

Tables

2.1 Current Mission, Goals, and Strategy of TTP 41

2.2 Humanities Preparatory Academy Fairness Committee 48

3.1 Developmental and Conceptual Framework for Human Rights
Education 56

3.2 Theoretical Underpinnings of Human Rights Education
Scholarship 64

4.1 Content and Pedagogy of the IHRE Textbooks 86

4.2 Content of HRLE Fourteen-Day Course 91

Acknowledgments

There are many people to thank for their assistance and support with this book. We would like to particularly thank Mark Richardson of Bloomsbury for his support of this book, as well as the new book series on peace and human rights education. Eunice Roh and Kate Walters, undergraduate students at Vassar College, helped compile the book and Further Reading List. Sophie Kennen and Grace Han assisted greatly with editing and formatting. Vassar students Kevin Arce, Natalie Bober, Grace Han, Stephen Han, Adam Weil, and Alice Woo conceptualized and created the Possibility Tree, and Grace and Stephen were instrumental in updating all of the graphics and figures in the book. Maria Autrey and Jazzmin Gota, doctoral students in International and Multicultural Education at the University of San Francisco, also offered important assistance with several components of the book, including formatting tables and figures, assisting with the further reading list, and developing the index. We'd like to extend our gratitude to all of our friends and colleagues—there are too many to name and you know who you are—but our work is stronger because of you! We do want to give a special shout out to our friends Lesley Bartlett, Colette Cann, Brooke Harris-Garad, David Ragland, Roozbeh Shirazi, Hakim Williams, and Zeena Zakharia for being our sounding board for ideas related to this book and other projects.

Maria: This book is the fruit of countless conversations over the years with my dear friend and colleague Monisha Bajaj. I am so grateful we crossed paths so many years ago and built such a strong relationship together. I am a better thinker, writer, and person for it! My writing accountability group also deserves great appreciation. Thank you, Dana Wright, Lionel Howard, Tara Brown, and Emma Sterrett-Hong, who read drafts and offered critical, loving feedback! As always, I owe so much to the people who came before me (including my parents, Peter and Chris), who stay with me (including my partner, Johnny Farraj), and who come after me (including my children, Dalia and Ziyad). The last few years have been filled with turmoil, uncertainly, grief, growth, community, and change, and whether or not you are here physically, mentally, or spiritually, you remain my guides and lights through it all.

Monisha: It has been such a privilege and pleasure to work together with Maria since we met nearly two decades ago in graduate school. This collaborative book allowed us to deepen our thinking in new and productive ways. And I always cherish the opportunity to spend more time together, in-person, on the phone, or zooming while engrossed in a shared document. An early conceptualization of Chapter 5 began during participation in a thematic residency on youth agency at the Rockefeller Foundation Bellagio Center; I extend my gratitude to the Center and to the fellow participants for the space to explore these ideas that enriched Maria and my subsequent collective work on the book. I would also like to especially thank my spouse, Bikku Kuruvila; our son, Kabir; and our parents for their support and love, especially as the final phase of writing this book took place during our time at home, with a global pandemic underway.

Copyright and Note on the Text

The authors have drawn from and adapted sections of the following previously published pieces for this book.

Bajaj, M., & Hantzopoulos, M. (Eds.). (2016), *Peace education: International perspectives.* New York and London: Bloomsbury.

Bajaj, M. (2018), Conceptualizing transformative agency in education for peace, human rights & social justice. *International Journal of Human Rights Education* 2(1): 1–22.

Bajaj, M., & Mabona, N. (2021), Theories of human rights education in comparative international education: From declarations to new directions. In T. Jules, R. Shields, & M. Thomas (Eds.), *Bloomsbury handbook of theory in comparative and international education.* London: Bloomsbury.

Bajaj, M. (2017), Human rights education for social change: Experiences from South Asia. In K. Bickmore, R. Hayhoe, C. Manion, K. Mundy, & R. Read (Eds.), *Comparative and international education: Issues for teachers* (2nd edn). Toronto: Canadian Scholars Press.

Bajaj, M. (2017), Introduction. In M. Bajaj (Ed.), *Human rights education: Theory, research, praxis.* Philadelphia: University of Pennsylvania Press.

Hantzopoulos, M. (2011), Deepening democracy: How one school's fairness committee offers an alternative to "Discipline". Reprinted with permission from *Rethinking Schools* in *Schools: Studies in Education*, 8(1): 112–16.

Hantzopoulos, M. (2013), The possibilities of restorative justice in US public schools: A case study of the fairness committee at a small NYC high school. *The Prevention Researcher*, 20(1): 7–10.

Hantzopoulos, M., Zakharia, Z., & Harris-Garad, B. (2021), Peace theories. In T. Jules, R. Shields, & M. Thomas (Eds.), *Bloomsbury handbook of theory in comparative and international education.* London: Bloomsbury.

Hantzopoulos, M., & Williams, H. (2017), Peace education as a field. In Michael A. Peters (Ed.), *Encyclopedia of educational philosophy and theory.* Singapore: Springer.

Hantzopoulos, M. (2016), *Restoring dignity in public schools: Human rights education in action.* New York: Teachers College.

Abbreviations

BRAC	Formerly an acronym for the Bangladesh Rural Advancement Committee, now Building Resources Across Communities
BIPOC	Black, Indigenous, and other People of Color
UNCAT	United Nations Convention Against Torture
CEDAW	The Convention on the Elimination of All Forms of Discrimination Against Women
CEP	Community Empowerment Program
UNCRC	United Nations Convention on the Rights of the Child
CREDD	Collective of Researchers on Educational Disappointment and Desire
GCE	Global citizenship education
GED	General Educational Development
HRE	Human rights education
HRLE	Human rights and legal education
HRLS	Human rights and legal services
IHRE	Institute for Human Rights Education
IIPE	International Institute of Peace Education
IRE	Indigenous rights education
NESRI	National Economic and Social Rights Initiative
NYC	New York City
NGOS	Nongovernmental organizations

OHCHR	United Nations Office of the High Commissioner for Human Rights
P–12	Preschool to Grade 12 educational settings
THRED	Transformative human rights education
TTP	Truth Telling Project
UDHR	Universal Declaration of Human Rights
UN	United Nations
UNDHRET	United Nations Declaration on Human Rights Education and Training
UNESCO	United Nations Educational, Scientific and Cultural Organization
UNICEF	United Nations Children's Fund
US	United States
USSR	Union of Soviet Socialist Republics
WWI	First World War
WWII	Second World War

Introduction

Chapter Outline

The "Possibility" Tree as a Metaphor for the Interconnected Fields of Peace and Human Rights Education	2
The Possibility Tree	6
Goals and Structure of Book	11

Over the past five decades, peace education and human rights education have moved out of the margins and have emerged distinctly and separately as global fields of scholarship and practice. While it was quite common for these formerly obscure fields to be somewhat peripheral to other more mainstream forms of education or scholarship (to the extent that some people have never heard of them), the terms "peace" and "human rights education" are no longer as ancillary as they used to be. Promoted through multiple efforts, including through the United Nations (UN), civil society, grassroots educators, in preschool to grade 12 (P–12) educational settings, and in the academe, both of these fields consider content, processes, and educational structures that seek to dismantle various forms of violence, as well as move toward broader cultures of peace, justice, and human rights. Though these two fields have developed independently, their growing presence in movements, scholarship, and educational settings has often raised questions not only about what each is but also about how they are distinct and similar.

The genesis of this book, and ultimately this new book series on Peace and Human Rights Education that this book launches, came about after multiple conversations between the two authors and among their colleagues and students about the similarities and differences in the fields. As both of us are scholars whose work and teaching not only engages these fields separately, but also bridges them, we decided that this introductory primer could help untangle the core concepts that define both fields, unpacking their histories, conceptual foundations, models and practices, and scholarly production. Moreover, we also consider the overlap between them to produce fertile ground for new engagement across the fields. As a result, *Educating for Peace and Human Rights: An Introduction* examines the nexus of these fields and provides a review of the scholarly research on the challenges and possibilities of implementing peace and human rights education in diverse global sites. While these fields are distinct, with their own unique bodies of literature, genealogies, epistemologies, and practices, their intersections provide a bridge for those whose work rests at the nexus and view it as a launching point for more robust critical engagement and work.

The "Possibility" Tree as a Metaphor for the Interconnected Fields of Peace and Human Rights Education

At the heart of much of the work of peace and human rights education across contexts is both reflective and ongoing engagement and praxis, and the possibilities of imagining and working toward more just and sustainable futures. While we explore more deeply the theoretical foundations of each field in subsequent chapters, we note here that the work and pedagogy of the late Brazilian scholar Paulo Freire in particular—rooted in critical consciousness, dialogical relationships and practice, transformative agency, and problem-posing—are often vehicles for the enactment of peace and human rights education. While Freire (1970/2000) employed several types of dynamic pedagogical tools in popular education (participatory research and action, culture circles, generative word mapping, etc.), one of the methods used for problem-posing was the "problem tree." The problem tree is a heuristic or visual device that allows people to explore the root causes of a particular issue that affects their daily lives by mapping these causes in relation to quotidian experiences and larger systemic policies and practices.

By making and visualizing the connections between one's lived experiences and structural framings, the book aims to put forward the idea that people in communities can collectively come up with ways to transform their social worlds toward a more just and humane future. Though we take up some of the post-structural critiques of Freire in later chapters, we note here the potential dynamic and cyclical nature of Freirean processes that engage local actors and are critical to its enactment, is oft disregarded or overlooked in these very critiques (see Hantzopoulos 2015). In many ways, the process of creating a problem tree is one that not only invites local engagement but also encourages local analyses and solutions to local problems, while simultaneously connecting them to larger structural and systemic issues others are also facing. Overall, the problem tree activity is concerned with both the process and the product, and sees these two threads as intertwined.

The work of urban educational and Indigenous studies scholar Eve Tuck (2009; 2012) with New York City (NYC) youth and other local stakeholders is a recent and illustrative example of how the problem tree can be deployed in both conceptualizing and mapping issues, and in this case, with their experiences with NYC public schools. The Collective of Researchers on Educational Disappointment and Desire (CREDD), which Tuck documents in her work, was formed to conduct youth participatory action research on New York City public school policies and practices that produce school push-out (see www.evetuck.com). As part of their work, they undertook mapping a problem tree about how and why their school system wasn't working for them. In the reproducible tree they created, one can visually see how the roots, trunks, branches, and leaves all give a full generative picture of why NYC schools are not working from the perspective of folks (students) who are ostensibly recipients of that system (Figure I.1).

To elaborate on the process of creating this tree, the researchers first explain how this method begins by identifying the problem and then they explain the visual and conceptual process.

> In the research project we conducted with the Youth Researchers for a New Education System, we used the problem, "The current school system isn't working." The leaves then describe the day-to-day occurrences of the problem, which are the symptoms of the problem. Examples of the leaves might include *my teacher told me not to come to class if I was going to be late, we have to share textbooks,* and *I have never met with my guidance counselor.* Next as a whole group we draw on patterns in the leaves to answer the question, "What feeds the leaves?" in order to start mapping the trunk. The trunk represents the attitudes or beliefs that keep the symptoms in play. Examples of ripples of the trunk might include *there aren't enough seats for all of the students in my classes, resources are unfairly distributed,* and *the generally held fear of young people in the US.* We then ask the question, "What roots the trunk?" in order to map the roots of the problem. The roots are the systemic and structural sources of the trunk ripples and the leaves. The roots might include *capitalism* and *hierarchical power systems of domination.* (http://www.evetuck.com/problem-tree)

The researchers of the CREDD project not only adapted this method to conceptually map systemic issues in NYC public schools but also used this

THE CURRENT NYC SCHOOl

"Problem Tree" Identifies Root Causes & Illu

CLASSROOMS ARE CROWDED, SECURITY IS STRICT, BUT THERE ARE STILL FIGHTS

THERE ARE TOO MANY RACIAL BORDERS/BARRIERS IN MY SCHOOL

WRITING ON THE WALLS AND ON THE DESKS

STUDENTS ARE DROPPING OUT

SCHOOLS HAV DIFFERENT RESOURCES BA ON LOCATION & NEIGHBORHO

TOO MUCH HOME WORK IS GIVEN

2nd GRADERS CUT CLASS

THERE'S NO SOAP IN THE BATHROOMS

GYM IS LESS FUN THAN MATH!

LACK OF RESPECT FOR THE CLASSROOM

SCHOOL IS A FASHION RUNWAY

CL W POINT FOR N

NO SCHOOL BANDS

COMPUTER CLASS WITH NO COMPUTERS ('TYPING' ON A PIECE OF PAPER)

NEED BETTER FOOD THAT IS ACCESSIBLE TO ALL STUDENTS

RESOURCES ARE NOT TAKEN CARE OF

THE STANDARD CURRICULUM DOESN'T MATCH MY REALITY

CLASSES WITH MISLEADING TITLES SOUND NIFTY BUT ARE CIRCUSES

CLASSES ARE OVER-FILLED WHILE OTHERS HAVE FEWER THAN TEN STUDENTS

FOOD IS DISGUSTING, LUNCH TASTES SO HORRIBLE, I END UP NOT EATING

PURPOSE OF MYSTERIO

STUDENT RELATIONSHIPS

I WANTED ART BUT MY GRADES SUCKED

THE D.O.E. MAKES CHANGES BASED ON HOW THEY THINK IT SHOULD BE, NOT WHAT WE NEED

THERE IS NO LOGIC TO HOW RESOURCES ARE ALLOCATED

SCHOOL IS OVER CROWDED

MATERIAL CONDITIONS

WHAT FEEDS

THERE IS NO VARIETY OF CLASSES IN MY MAJOR

ADMINISTRATION SCHOOL RULES & POLICIES

FEAR OF YOUNG PEOPLE

SO CON

TOO MUCH WORK FROM OLD DUSTY TEXT BOOKS WITH PAGES STUCK TOGETHER INSTEAD OF TEACHERS TEACHING US

TEACHERS BEING BUDDIES WITH STUDENTS AT THE EXPENSE OF EDUCATION AND RESPECT

YOUTH ARE CONSIDERED OPEN TARGETS FOR HUMILIATION

RESOURCES ARE UNFAIRLY ALLOCATED

A

TEACHERS VERY RARELY ANSWER QUESTIONS

STAFF: ATTITUDES & DISRESPECT

TEACHER

EXTER (MAYORAL CONT

STAFF ARE AGEIST, AND USE THIS TO MAKE US FEEL POWERLESS

TEACHERS DISRESPECT STUDENTS & GET AWAY WITH IT

TEACHERS DON'T CARE LIKE THEY USED TO

MISUSE OF AUTHORITY

RACISM

TEACHERS ENGAGING IN SEXUAL ACTS WITH STUDENTS

TEACHERS ARE VERY RUDE

LACK OF MUTUAL RESPECT BETWEEN TEACHERS & STUDENTS

TEACHERS TREAT STUDENTS LIKE WE'RE STUPID

TEACHERS DON'T CARE IF WE PASS

WE HAVE TO COMPETE FO HAVE RIGHTS TO; EVERYTHING

ART: BE RIVERA, 2008

A BELIEF THAT POWER/KNOWLEDGE COMES FROM THE TOP, SO THE BEST WAY TO DO THINGS IS TOP DOWN

WHAT ARE

PEOPLE ARE DISEMPOWERED

"Problem Tree" is a result of Project P.I.E.S. (Progressively Investigating Education Solutio

Figure 0.1 CREDD Problem Tree.

as an approach to "collaboratively generate research questions, as part of our participatory design of research projects, as a tool of data collection in focus groups, and as a tool to facilitate collective analysis of myriad data" (www.evetuck.com/problemtree). Problem trees are therefore not only simply utilized to describe problems; they also function as community-led dialogues or conversations, and can be used as a springboard to generate critical consciousness and inspire new ways of imagining more just and inclusive spaces. By focusing on how one's lived experiences intersect and are shaped by larger systemic issues, they can be used as a point of departure to consider contextualized approaches that move toward dismantling oppressive structures and creating new ways of being in the world.

The Possibility Tree

Inspired by the visual aspect of the problem tree (which helps map the structural roots and the quotidian realities that manifest from injustice individuals and communities face), we decided to flip this model to map a "possibility tree"—one that both conceptualizes and delineates the ways in which peace and human rights education might be intertwined, providing a visual catalyst for imagining new worlds and possibilities. We use this visual, titled Educating for Peace and Human Rights Possibility Tree (see Figure 5.1), as a heuristic in Chapter 5 to illustrate these points after we have mapped these fields separately in earlier chapters. We then offer a framework in that chapter for how educational visions can grow out of the common, shared soil of liberatory education projects, such as peace education and human rights education. Thus, while we make note of this here, we explain and bring this tree to the forefront in Chapter 5 when we discuss in depth some of the intersections of the field.

Nonetheless, we were also inspired by the *process* of making the possibility tree as a means to illustrate and model some of the fundamentally fluid and generative pedagogies undergirding critical approaches to peace and human rights education. In order to embody both the spirit and the heart of this process rather than just impose only our own understandings in this introductory chapter, we decided to also include a possibility tree made with Maria's former undergraduate-level students after they took the course "Education for Peace, Justice, and Human Rights" at Vassar College. We decide to share their work here in the introduction to both show how local meanings shape people's perceptions of peace, justice, and human rights and model the dynamic process.

Reflecting a similar process as Tuck (2009), the students mapped out the roots, trunks, branches, and leaves to obtain a more thorough understanding of the fields and their relationships to each other by considering "What does a culture of peace, justice, and human rights look like?" This process took place during several meetings outside of class in the fall of 2019 over the course of two months, and Maria (the instructor) only provided the prompts and questions. The group of undergraduate students—Kevin Arce, Natalie Bober, Grace Han, Alice Woo, and Adam Weil—took the process from there to flesh this out over time and met on their own without Maria. While they all were undergraduate students at Vassar at the time and shared a lens that was certainly influenced by that context, they all also have different lived experiences both on campus and off, rooted in their cultural, racialized, socioeconomic, migration, sexual, religious, and gendered identities. They eventually came up with the visual in Figure I.2, with the help of another student, Stephen Han.

The mapping process revolved around a few questions and prompts. In order to articulate the "roots," the group was asked, "What are the roots of a culture of peace, justice, and human rights?" The group not only grappled with this over time and ultimately expressed some of the foundational "core" of peace education and human rights education, but also some of the basic structures that they believed would encourage such a culture to flourish. As indicated in the tree, these roots included fundamental concepts to both fields like equity, planetary stewardship, global citizenship, positive peace, human rights, demilitarization, decolonization, and more. For the trunk, we kept the question "What feeds the symptoms?" to articulate mechanisms and vehicles to promote and "feed" these foundational roots. As noted earlier, these included education, the eradication of direct violence, the enactment of positive peace, and people protesting for social change. While the group did not name notions like critical consciousness, transformative agency, or even peace and human rights education (just education), their symptoms often implicitly relied on these processes through the ways they relate to the roots and the branches. In other words, there was an assumption of what education truly should be (to inherently embody these concepts) when looking at the tree as an interconnected (and not isolated) whole.

To articulate what would be listed in the branches, the group decided to build off the "nourishment" from the symptoms and describe how this might

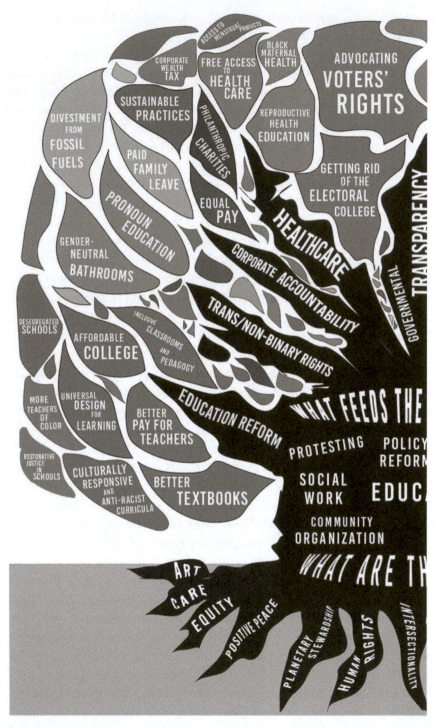

Figure 0.2 Envisioning a Culture of Peace, Justice, and Human Rights Possibility Tree.

manifest in policy and practice; thus, included are concepts like health care, redistribution of wealth, and so on. The leaves then become the articulations of these concepts and more specifically, how these policies manifest in individuals' and communities' lived experiences. There is a range of possibilities expressed, including voter rights, paid family leave, and affordable housing. Moreover, one can see how each branch/vehicle leads to the possible lived experience—the branches and subsequent leaves were color-coded in the original (reproduced in grayscale here) to show how the branches nurture the leaves.

While the tree is partial and not complete, is contextually situated and bound, can be expanded with more additions and definitions, and can even be contested, it shows the pedagogy of peace and human rights education in action, both in process and as a "work-in-progress" product (as it is something that can be remade and shifted over time). As well, the tree visually presents ways to view how these two fields might interlock foundationally—despite their distinct characteristics—which is the crux of the arguments developed in this book. Though we grapple with some of the divergent and intersecting theoretical foundations that promote and/or hinder cultures of peace and human rights in the book, this is a visual to map what could/does exist and, in many ways, provides an opening to what we explore more deeply. While this is not a complete metaphor for all of the linkages and themes raised between the two fields in the book, we hope that this possibility tree—as a work-in-progress product—sparks some conversations about how these visions are entangled.

The problem tree activity, conceptualized by Freire as a means to understand the root causes of forms of violence and oppression, can be paired well with the possibility tree activity, where, once problems are identified and discussed, new practices and ways of being can be imagined and brought into focus to spur necessary action. We hope that this example also inspires students, groups, and communities to craft their own trees, tailored to their own hopes, dreams, and visions, utilizing or modifying the initial prompt around cultures of peace, justice, and human rights. Such efforts can help "pluriversalize human rights education and peace education" in order to "recognize and include forms of knowledge that have been subjugated by modernity and coloniality, . . . and to advance epistemic justice" (Zembylas 2020). With many trees of possibility sprouting across context, they can offer needed oxygen to fuel our efforts, movements, and imaginations toward envisioning greater peace and justice.[1]

Goals and Structure of Book

The purpose and goals of this book are multifold. While we seek to introduce readers to the fields of peace and human rights education, address key questions that come from those fields, and deepen knowledge for those that are already familiar with the fields, we also want to help readers understand more clearly the contours of and overlap between the fields. As a result, there are three related overarching goals of the book: (1) to highlight the distinct evolutions of peace education and human rights education around the globe; (2) to underscore the ways in which these two fields converge and work in tandem with each other to produce related scholarship and practice; and (3) to launch an innovative series with Bloomsbury that will advance these fields (separately and collectively) through case studies, empirical research, and monographs that enhance the theories and conceptual terrain of these fields.

This book offers readers a chance to deeply understand the fields of peace education and human rights education as they have developed on their own including in their normative, critical, and decolonial dimensions, as well as see the linkages between the fields. This book also lays a foundation for the subsequent books in the series that will feature global case studies and/or groundbreaking conceptual contributions to these fields. It also sets forth a comprehensive research agenda outlined in Chapter 6 (and provides a robust annotated bibliography in the Appendix) for undergraduate and graduate-level students, as well as for community-based scholars and practitioners, to situate their work within larger ongoing conversations in the fields.

Beyond the introduction, this book is organized as follows. Chapter 1 provides a broad overview of the field of peace education. In particular, we highlight its history and development as a field, considering the conceptual and philosophical underpinnings of how "peace" has been understood by peace education scholars and practitioners. We further explore the various models associated with its practice, the ways in which the field has become legitimized and operationalized, and the relevant scholarship and case studies that have helped define it. We chart the ways that different waves of scholarship have moved from more Eurocentric and Western ideas about peace and peace education to more critical and decolonial approaches that espouse more epistemic diversity in the field.

Chapter 2 then provides more context through two case studies about the enactment of peace education, highlighting the ways in which anti-racist restorative and transformational justice initiatives in the United States (US) intersect with many of the theories, purposes, and goals of peace education, including in its critical and postcolonial (and dynamic) forms. The chapter considers how two justice-based initiatives—The Truth Telling Project (TTP) based in St. Louis, Missouri, and restorative practices based in NYC schools— might engage and move communities toward worlds that seek to dismantle white supremacy and racial violence and toward just visions of peace. Together, the cases give the reader a small window into what organic and context-specific peace education initiatives might look like from the ground up, rather than being imposed from above. As well, given the uprisings against police violence and anti-Blackness that have erupted in the United States since initially writing this chapter, and the subsequent policy discussions and changes that they are inspiring (redirecting police funding, moving police presence out of schools), these windows illuminate how the collective and sometimes slow work on the ground can be catalysts for larger social change.

Chapter 3 is quite similar to Chapter 1, tracing human rights education in ways that the earlier chapter did for peace education (provides a broad overview of the field of human rights education and also highlights its history and development as a field, considering the conceptual underpinnings, the various models associated with its practice, the ways in which the field has become legitimized and operationalized, and the relevant scholarship and case studies that have helped definite it). We also examine in Chapter 3 decolonial critiques of normative human rights vis-à-vis their influence on scholarship in human rights education.

Chapter 4 then explores how human rights education (HRE) as a global educational movement is taken up locally by educators, activists, and nongovernmental organizations (NGOs) in South Asia and zooms in on two examples of transformative human rights education in the South Asian context that seek—in different locally contextualized ways—to interrogate power asymmetries and offer members of marginalized groups the opportunity to envision and demand equal rights. While the two cases (People's Watch and BRAC) are different in approach, population and context, both programs rely on well-trained teachers/facilitators who use innovative curricula, effective participatory pedagogies, and strong relationships with learners to assist them in recognizing and confronting the injustices that surround their lives. Similar to the peace education case studies that explore one school-based and one nonformal community education approach, Chapter 4 also reviews a school-based and a community-based model to highlight our arguments throughout this book that peace and human rights education can be taken up in classrooms, community spaces, museums, families, outdoors, and elsewhere.

Chapter 5 considers the ways in which peace education and human rights education converge, intersect, and diverge. While Chapters 1 and 3 trace the genealogies of these fields distinctly from each other so that their unique origins and trajectories are mapped out, the goal of this chapter is to understand the fertile terrain in which the fields overlap so that keen new theoretical insights and framings can emerge. This intersection is the heart of the book—the intertwined roots of our tree of possibility (Figure 5.1)—illustrating the ways that the fields merge together, at times more clearly than not, to help us map and understand new ways forward.

The concluding chapter considers future scholarship and a research agenda at the bridge of the two fields described in the previous chapters. Our goal is to help create more robust conceptual frameworks for engagement, which are needed to address the myriad social justice issues facing the planet at this time. Finally, we provide an extensive annotated bibliography of major and seminal texts in both peace and human rights education. The purpose of this section is to provide readers with an overview of the bodies of literature that have defined the fields.

We hope that this book offers an informed starting point for newcomers to the fields—to see their similarities, connections, and differences—as well as an opportunity for reflection for those already embedded within them to conceptualize the work in new ways. Paulo Freire noted, more than half a century ago, "Education either functions as an instrument . . . to bring about conformity or it becomes the practice of freedom, the means by which [people] . . . discover how to participate in the transformation of their world" (1970/2000: 125). As we consider the global and local challenges of our time—the problems and possibilities, their intersections and their particularities—we are inspired by the potential of peace and human rights education, while knowing, embracing, and grappling with its limitations, as a space for visioning, imagining, and working toward a more just and sustainable future.

Peace Education

The Foundations and Future Directions of a Field[1]

Chapter Outline

From Theory to Practice: The Development of Peace
Education over Time   17
Major Pedagogical Influences in Peace Education   21
Mainstreaming the Field: Integrating Peace Education
into Schools and Beyond   25
New Directions and Ways Forward: Critical Peace Education,
Post-Structural Influences, and Decolonial Approaches   27
Conclusion   32

In the last several decades, peace education has become a recognized field that has emerged from the margins of educational policy and practice to become increasingly established in various educational settings worldwide. Once a rather obscure or unheard-of practice in mainstream educational circles, peace education is now commonly integrated into education and peacebuilding efforts adopted by international organizations, UN agencies, ministries of education, local and global nongovernmental organizations (NGOs), and other types of educational institutions, including grassroots movements for community justice and activism. Overall, peace education is a wide-ranging field of practice and scholarship that is viewed as a vehicle both to undo violence in its various forms (e.g., direct, cultural, and structural) and to build conditions for sustainable peace (see also, Hantzopoulos, Zakharia, and Harris-Garad 2021). Considering its range and origins across the globe, peace education is understandably rife with plural and multiple interpretations and enactments. Informed by diverse philosophies, epistemologies, theories, traditions, and practices, peace education cannot be bound and reduced a singular definition (Bajaj 2008; Bajaj & Hantzopoulos 2016; Bar-Tal 2002; Danesh 2006; Hantzopoulos 2011).

Nonetheless, most scholars of peace education agree on some key tenets of theory and practice that ground the field, and there is general consensus that peace education is mainly concerned with both dismantling all forms of violence and considering ways to create and maintain a more just and peaceful world (Bajaj & Hantzopoulos 2016). Driven by the teleological concept of "peace," peace education research and practice draws from the field of peace studies to consider and imagine a world in which all forms of violence are absent, and positive and negative peace fuse to form comprehensive peace (Reardon 2000). Though discussed later in the chapter, negative peace assumes the absence of direct violence like war or torture, whereas positive peace assumes the cessation of structural violence so that societal conditions allow for justice and equity to prevail (Galtung 1969). Peace education, therefore, in its distinct manifestations worldwide, considers how practice, theory, and pedagogy combine to develop the necessary skills and ideologies to envision and move toward a more equitable, just, and nonviolent future (Bajaj 2008; Hantzopoulos 2011; Reardon 1988). While the argument that education can help eliminate all forms of violence is a site of considerable (and essential) debate, peace education research and practice pulls from these varied robust repertoires to consider how to dismantle violent structures in a variety of contexts and domains.

The following chapter considers more closely the concepts that define the field and its development in both theory and practice across the globe. Specifically, we trace the foundations, the histories, and the pedagogies that have informed the field, and consider competing theories and debates within it. We examine the normative conceptions of peace that have undergirded the field since its inception as well as the decolonial directions that scholars have increasingly taken in the past decade. We look at how other fields have informed its trajectories and examine the ways forward, privileging the perspectives of critical theorists, practitioners, and scholars.

From Theory to Practice: The Development of Peace Education over Time

As a field of study, peace education can trace its roots back to the early nineteenth century, though it discursively emerged more prominently in the post–Second World War period. At this time, many Western nations and peoples sought ways to prevent the large-scale wars that they had just experienced in the first half of that century (Harris 2008). Despite this emergence as a named field, peace education was not necessarily new, nor was it Western. Many non-Western and Indigenous societies were based in religious and spiritual teachings and traditions that sought to educate and lead people to more peaceful and just worlds (Harris 2004, 2008). Though violence always existed alongside teachings of peace, there is no question that peace studies, and by proxy peace education, have been informed by these myriad traditions.

The proliferation of peace education in Western Europe paralleled both the growth of peace movements and the realities of increased intra-nation strife and class conflict at that time (Harris 2008). For instance, in the nineteenth century, the development of peace movements within civil society was in direct response to increased armament (from the wars that defined that century), mass industrialization (resulting in wealth disparities and class conflict), and eventually the rise of the nation-state (which led to internal civil strife, alliances, and borders among nations). Further, Europe was also engaged in inhumane violence outside of its "borders" through the colonization of Africa, Asia, the Caribbean, and Latin America, and its active and continued participation in the trans-Atlantic slave trade. In other words, the growth of peace movements in parts of Europe concurrently surfaced during some of its darkest and most violent times (Hantzopoulos & Williams 2017). Moreover, in other regions of the world, peace movements and related educational approaches developed and flourished in their localized contexts often in direct opposition to European imperial brutality (see also, Hantzopoulos, Zakharia, & Harris 2021).

While the development of peace education in the twentieth century takes multiple forms and pathways contingent upon specific geographical and historical contexts, the contradiction of looming and increased direct, structural, and cultural violence worldwide continued to thrust peace studies and peace education forward as fields. According to Harris (2008), the period before and immediately after the First World War (WWI) brought forth more peace activity from macro-level entities through the establishment of the Nobel Peace Prize in 1895 and the formation of the League of Nations in 1920. Paradoxically, this peace activity occurred during an era when much of Europe not only remained committed to maintaining colonial power beyond its borders, but also was contending with the steady rise of fascism from within. Within Europe, segments of the population questioned the dominant realist frameworks of "peace through war or armament" that framed the previous century and led to a colossal war, and began to consider how peace might be achieved through justice, nonviolence, and equality. It was during this time that disarmament movements and societies started to form, and in some cases, peace education began to be integrated informally and formally in schools. Specifically, teachers started to adopt a more global lens by interweaving international relations within the social studies curriculum, explicitly considering with students how inter- and intra-national cooperation might contribute to a more peaceful world order (Harris & Morrison 2003).

Progressive educational theories, developed and influenced by educational and social activists like Maria Montessori, John Dewey, and Jane Addams, also emerged more distinctly during the early twentieth century and in this intra–World War period. While schools historically had generally inculcated narrow nationalist views that reified a perceived "Other," these theories explicitly began to view schools as potential sites to promote shared humanity instead. By emphasizing shared community, democracy, and interdependence over individualism and self-interest, and transcending national and regional borders, these theories sought to prevent marginalization, violence, and wars through education. Unfortunately, the Second World War (WWII) ushered in the worst of rigid nationalism; yet, there was a renewed commitment to world peace and global citizenry in its wake. This push was most obviously evident in the formation of the United Nations in 1945 and bolstered by the adoption of the Universal Declaration of Human Rights (UDHR) in 1948 as a foundational document of the new global organization (Harris 2008; Reardon 2000). The UDHR's preamble integrally links human rights to peace, stating that "Whereas recognition of the inherent dignity and of the equal and inalienable rights of all members of the human family is the foundation of freedom, justice and peace in the world" (1948).

The development of peace movements, nonviolent approaches, and peace education was greatly influenced by the heightened visibility of global movements for decolonization, freedom, liberation, and self-determination in both the Global South and among marginalized populations in the Global North at this time. In India, Gandhi honed his theories and practices of nonviolence that ultimately led to Indian independence from British rule, inspiring others globally to fight for liberation through nonviolent tactics and launching an entire field known as Gandhian studies (see Bajaj 2016a). Anticolonial uprisings worldwide followed similar paths. According to Hantzopoulos & Williams (2017):

> From the Civil Rights Movement in the United States to anti-apartheid organizing in South Africa, many movements began to adopt non-violent, direct action approaches as a central tool for decolonization and liberation. While not all movements against colonial, neo-colonial, settler-colonial and imperial empires at the time were non-violent, many of these uprisings resulted in more socially just practices under new regimes that emphasized positive peace through literacy campaigns, social and national welfare programs, public health and equitable housing policies. (p. 2)

Peace education research and practice was truly indebted to these radical visions and considerations of alternative ways of being and living more justly in the world.

The emergence of the Cold War, the nuclear arms race, and the threat of nuclear war between the Union of Soviet Socialist Republics (USSR) and the United States (US) in the 1970s and 1980s launched new peace movements globally that were centered on nuclear disarmament. Geopolitical and international relations at the time were still grounded in realist notions of world order, and the interests of the nation-state to provide security and protection of citizens *within* their respective borders served as the catalyst and rationale for state-decision-making. The nuclear arms race and the threat of nuclear war between the USSR and the United States (and the involvement of allied nations on either side) was a direct result of such realist political thinking. However, this was in direct conflict with cosmopolitan beliefs that considered a more global approach to human (rather than national) security that is grounded in morality and ethics. Snauwaert (2008) argues that realist notions of peace, like those that were defined during the Cold War, are bereft of morals, whereas comprehensive peace is contingent upon a cosmopolitan moral order in which all human beings—regardless of constructed borders—view and accept the inherent dignity of the other.

In response to such developments and the real threat of global annihilation, academics and scholars began to establish peace research projects, framed by opposing concepts of peace and violence, that helped codify peace studies as an academic field. Specifically, it was during the Cold War and in the wake of the Korean and Vietnam wars when Norwegian sociologist and leading peace theorist Johan Galtung (1976) began to distinguish between and among different forms of violence to conceptualize various types of peace (Harris 2004). Initially, peace research focused on direct violence, both personal and large-scale, defining peace as the absence of violence and war. This type of peace—negative peace—was explicitly concerned with security, or stopping violence from happening. In other words, negative peace is in response to direct violence with an identifiable perpetrator. This includes actions like a ceasefire after a war, treaties among nations, or the development of security or defense apparatuses, or interpersonally, preventing physical or behavioral violence toward one another.

Peace research, however, began to shift at this time to reflect on the root and structural causes of violence. This turn led to more nuanced understandings of violence beyond its obvious direct and physical forms to consider how a genuinely peaceful world might be realized (Galtung 1969). For instance, while the concept of direct violence included how physical, behavioral, or direct violence affected individuals, groups, or nations, Galtung explored other dimensions of violence, including structural, cultural, and political, to shed light on the obstacles to truly achieving peace. For instance, structural violence considered how social and economic systems produced inequity in societies and communities; political violence considered how opposition forces are silenced, marginalized, and abused; and cultural violence examined how groups of people are "denied dignity, rights, and opportunities based on their ascribed identities to bolster racism, patriarchy, militarism, classism, and other forms of systemic oppression" (Hantzopoulos & Williams 2017: 3).

While all these forms of violence are interrelated and often overlap, distinguishing among them led to more robust definitions of peace. By centering systemic forms of violence, peace researchers introduced the concept of positive peace, which relies not only on the absence of direct violence but also the pursuit of justice, human rights, and societal well-being. Thus, comprehensive peace could only be attained through the pursuit of both domains—negative and positive peace (Reardon 1988, 2000). Galtung (1976) further identified five large-scale problems that interfered with the attainment of comprehensive peace, which included (1) direct violence or war, (2) inequality, (3) injustice, (4) environmental degradation, and (5) alienation. He argued that a genuinely peaceful world could only be attained when nonviolence, economic welfare, social justice, ecological balance, and civic participation were realized.

Peace research was also greatly strengthened by feminist scholarship in the 1970s and 1980s that examined the inextricable relationships among violence, militarism, and patriarchy. Scholars like Birgit Brock-Utne (1989) and Betty Reardon (1985, 1988, 2000) produced groundbreaking work that argued that peace—both positive and negative—necessitated a gendered lens that aimed to dismantle patriarchy, and subsequently eradicate enduring direct and structural violence. Their analyses led to the importance of education, and specifically peace education, as a key component in helping to resocialize people and communities away from masculine ideals of militarism, war, competition, and violence toward more trusting, collaborative, peaceful, just, and sustainable futures (see also Harris 2004).

By the 1980s, peace education became more recognized and legitimized as an academic field, and the connections among peace research, peace movements, and peace education became stronger. Like its parent field of peace studies, peace education developed as a way to grapple with and work toward dismantling growing worldwide poverty alongside extreme wealth, the destruction of the environment, the persistence of violent conflicts, the increase in terrorism (including state-sponsored forms), and rampant racism, sexism, and xenophobia (Hantzopoulos & Williams 2017). Scholars and practitioners began to lay out frameworks and pathways to transform populations and societies from violent to peaceful. For example, scholars like Hicks (1988) outlined approaches to peace education through various realms, such as government strength, conflict mediation and resolution, personal peace, world order, and as power relationships. Reardon (1988) laid out the three conceptual pillars of the field: planetary stewardship, global citizenship, and humane relationships, as the basis to educate for peace. Together, these scholars began to identify the ways in which skills, knowledges, and attitudes, influenced by concepts identified in peace research, coalesced to form an interrelated foundation for peace education.

Major Pedagogical Influences in Peace Education

Peace education pedagogy, in relationship to its development as an academic field, was inspired and influenced by the works of many prominent educational theorists, like John Dewey (1916) and Maria Montessori (1949), already briefly mentioned, and Paulo Freire (1970/2000), whom we also discuss briefly in the introduction (Bajaj 2008, and Hantzopoulos & Williams 2017).[2] Their pedagogies and education approaches were not only less hierarchical and more student-centered and directed but also reflected broader visions for ways in which humans should interact with the earth, each other, and their broader communities more generally. For instance, Dewey's (1916) progressive and experiential educational pedagogy mainly focused on meaning-making, learning by doing, reflection on the experiences of learning, forging connections across disciplines, the consideration of context, and applicable and collaborative problem-solving. Yet, these approaches were also rooted in broader progressive ideals about democracy, society, and the world. Philosophically speaking, he was an instrumentalist who believed that ideas could be implemented to solve real-world problems. While initially Dewey believed that the use of force was sometimes necessary in ushering in democracy, he eventually shifted his thinking to connect education and peace, and that the promotion of internationalism could be a central check against the kind of insidious nationalism that fed war.

Dewey also firmly believed that rote memorization curtailed creative and imaginative thinking and viewed subjects such as geography and history as not just as the listing of mountains, towns, and cities or the enumeration of dates and key persons but as disciplines that needed to be taught with context and social meaning in mind. By teaching these subjects in such an experiential and interdisciplinary manner, he believed that students would forge more meaningful and interdependent connections between the material, themselves, and the world beyond. He thus advocated for experiential learning, where students would meld theory, reflection, and practice, and experience cooperative and integrated learning to build skills for democratic building and living. As a result, Dewey (1916) believed that education in this manner would also lead to a healthy and robust democracy that also fostered global connectivity and sustainable world peace (Howlett 2008).

Similarly, Montessori's pedagogical focus on children's passions and directions also related to larger concepts of peacebuilding and peaceful living that transcended time and place (Montessori 1916). Montessori's methodology and theory emerged out of her own scientific observations and experiments regarding the education of the "whole child." Like Dewey, she believed that learning needed to be integrated and not compartmentalized, but she also emphasized the key role of the child in this process. Specifically, she believed that students are natural learners and that teachers should be a guide in the classroom, allowing the child's passions and imagination to direct the learning (Montessori 1916). She also travelled the world advocating that values such as global citizenship and respect for diversity were just as central as math and science. Because she believed that child-directed pedagogy would foster independence and critically reflective thinking, she also concluded that these skills would build more cooperative relationships among students, their teachers, and their communities, and ultimately contribute to a more peaceful and democratic world (Duckworth 2008).

Further, by emphasizing the importance of work and play, Montessori's methods, and classrooms modeled on her methods, are highly structured. Her pedagogical methods include peer learning, self-assessment, experiential learning, adaptability, and communication, to strike a balance between the requisite characteristics of independence and interdependence that lead to individual empowerment, critical thinking, and cooperative living (Montessori 2016). With the teacher being decentered, learners become acclimatized to self-monitoring and intrinsic motivation. This modeling was fundamental to her larger vision because Montessori also argued that peace knowledges and content had to align with peace pedagogies and structures in order for learners to grasp more resolutely the tangibility of nonviolence and peace (Duckworth 2008; Hantzopoulos & Williams 2017).

Peace education pedagogy has also been greatly informed by Freire's (1970/2000) work, including his emphasis on reframing student-teacher relationships to be more egalitarian. Freire (1970/2000) believed that hierarchical student-teacher relationships mirrored the relationships of the oppressed and the oppressor. In particular, he critiqued the top-down concept of banking education and the idea that the teacher held all authority and knowledge and deposited this knowledge into the student, who was assumed to be a "blank slate." By equalizing both parties' role in the co-construction of knowledge, acknowledging that no knowledge is neutral, and valorizing what the "student" brings to the table, Freire (1970/2000) believed that student and teacher could not only work toward each other's liberation but also move toward a more just and equitable society grounded in collective freedom. Central to this process was the concept of problem-posing (conscientization) in which the "learner" critically reflects on their world, and the world around them, and then takes critical action to transform it. In this process, hierarchical relationships are flipped bottom-up to imagine new realities toward a more just and sustainable society. Freire's (1970/2000) explicit commitment to dismantling structural violence coincided with that same goal of peace education (Bartlett 2008; Hantzopoulos & Williams 2017) and is also threaded in transformative human rights education, as taken up later in the book.

While these theories often inspire peace education pedagogy, peace education in practice also relies on localized and contextual philosophical foundations. For example, the concept of *ubuntu*, a Nguni Bantu word meaning "humanity," informed a collectivist philosophy known as ubuntuism propagated by decolonial thinkers throughout parts of Southern sub-Saharan Africa when nations like Zimbabwe and South Africa transitioned to majority rule. For instance, *ubuntu* informed the spirit of South Africa's postapartheid national Truth and Reconciliation Commission, as defined by Nobel Peace Prize winner Desmond Tutu to mean

> my humanity is caught up, is inextricably bound up, in [others]. We belong in a bundle of life. We say, "a person is a person through other people." I am human because I belong, I participate, and I share. A person with ubuntu is open and available to others, affirming of others, does not feel threatened that others are able and good. (1999: 34–5)

Peace education scholar Murithi argues that *ubuntu* offers a framework that emphasizes a shared humanity through "a value system for giving and receiving forgiveness" and promoting reconciliation (2009: 227). Murithi further elucidates the relevance of *ubuntu* for peace educators stating that

> the vital lesson for peace education that ubuntu promotes is that the essential unity and interdependence of humanity must constantly be emphasized. By nurturing the reality of our shared humanity, this can serve as the foundation upon which to live out the principles which this unity suggests: empathy for others; the sharing of our common resources; and a collaborative approach to resolving our common problems. (2009: 230)

Other communities and regions similarly have philosophical traditions that highlight connection, reconciliation, and peacemaking. For example, the Indigenous Mayan concept of *In lak'ech*, translates as "I am you and you are me." For peace educators, finding philosophical resonance in seminal educational thinkers like Dewey, Freire, or Montessori, or philosophical concepts such as ubuntu or *In lak'ech*, has informed the ways that peace education pedagogy anchors its pedagogical orientations locally to promote critical thinking and consciousness.

Mainstreaming the Field: Integrating Peace Education into Schools and Beyond

With gaining prominence, peace education became associated with and connected to other fields and forms of educational justice movements that inherently intersected with the broader practices, pedagogies, and ideals of peace education, including human rights education, conflict resolution, environmental education, and multicultural and anti-racist education. Scholars began to point out the inherent linkages between peace education and these other forms of education, articulating that peace education is in some ways the connecting glue among other these other initiatives (Harris 2004, 2008; Hicks 1988). For instance, human rights education, which contends with the issue of human dignity, security, and the attainment of rights and entitlements, connected with the concepts of violence, nonviolence, and sustainable futures in peace education (Reardon 2000). As we discuss in Chapter 3, these linkages have often united the fields of peace and human rights education in which much of the research, practice, and scholarship overlap significantly.

The proliferation of conflict resolution programs in the 1980s also helped legitimize peace education as a necessary form of education. Given the spectre of nuclear war globally that defined those times, and the increasing interpersonal violence between and among children and youth in and out of schools, these programs became increasingly popular in schools and became an integral subset of peace education (Harris 2004). Similarly, the growth of multicultural and anti-racist education (Banks & Banks 1993; Gay 1994; Grant 1977; Grant & Sleeter 1986; Nieto & Bode 1992) as a means to address increasing xenophobia within and across nations and the unequal racialized realities of educational, health, and other social and public outcomes also intersected with the goals of peace education to eradicate structural violence and work toward positive peace.

Finally, while global concerns about environmental degradation, pollution, and the depletion of the earth's resources led to the fields of environmental studies and environmental education, peace education also addressed these concerns in its foundational premise of planetary stewardship as part of a just and sustainable peace (Reardon 1988). With the ongoing realities of extreme climate change and overwhelming natural disasters (exacerbated by human consumption, conflict, and way of life), peace education has reanchored ecological security as a fundamental part of the project (Harris & Morrison 2003; Harris 2004; Bajaj & Chiu 2009). Given its centrality across many subsets of other fields of education over time, some scholars have suggested that peace education should be a universal and integrated paradigm in any form of education going forward (Synott 2005) (Figure 1.1).

During the 1990s and into the 2000s, peace education moved beyond P–12 practice in schools to become integrated into college and university-level curricula that sought to prepare teachers. For example, peace education had gained traction as a field through the establishment of the International Institute on Peace Education (IIPE) at Teachers College, Columbia University, with its inaugural institute held there in 1982 (Jenkins 2008). While originally organized from New York, the IIPE has evolved into a biannual gathering held in different cities around the world for peace scholars, educators, and

Figure 1.1 Peace Education and Related Fields (modified from Bajaj & Chiu 2009).

activists. In facilitating exchanges of theory, practice, and pedagogy, the IIPE "operates as an applied peace education laboratory that provides a space for pedagogical experimentation; cooperative, deep inquiry into shared issues; and advancing theoretical, practical, and pedagogical applications."[3] It has had and continues to have a profound influence on the work of peace education scholars and activists worldwide.

The establishment of the IIPE and other peace education initiatives (i.e., the Hague Appeal for Peace, the Global Campaign for Peace Education, the Peace Boat) has also cultivated more fertile terrain for burgeoning peace educational scholarship and, in many ways, has opened doors for the institutionalization of peace education in the academy. One of IIPE's founders, Betty Reardon, also helped found a renowned graduate level specialization in peace education at Teachers College, Columbia University, four decades ago. In subsequent years, the University of Peace in Costa Rica and the European Peace University in Austria also began offering degrees and specializations in peace education. Although degrees in peace studies had been increasing since the 1970s, this new era legitimized peace education and its focus on training educators and scholars to help build a "culture of peace." The fruits of such efforts resulted in the international promotion of peace education, including with the United Nations Educational, Scientific and Cultural Organization (UNESCO) declaring a decade for the international promotion of peace and nonviolence from 2001 to 2010. Moreover, *The Journal of Peace Education* launched in 2004 and provided a forum for the production and dissemination of global peace education scholarship. As a result, prominent academic societies such as the American Educational Research Association and the Comparative and International Educational Society all formed robust special interest groups to promote the academic work emerging from the field (see also Hantzopoulos, Zakharia, and Harris-Garad 2021).

New Directions and Ways Forward: Critical Peace Education, Post-Structural Influences, and Decolonial Approaches

More recently, peace education practitioners and scholars working in diverse geographic and sociopolitical contexts have called for greater attention to "critical peace education," something that emerged in the 1970s but has been reinvigorated as an intentional and explicit approach to peace education in recent years (Bajaj 2008, 2015; Bajaj & Brantmeier 2011; Bajaj & Hantzopoulos 2016; Diaz-Soto 2005). Specifically, responding to post-structural and postcolonial critiques that raised questions about the universal, normative, and decontextualized foundational notions about peace and how to attain it (Gur-Ze'ev 2001; Hantzopoulos, 2010; Kester & Cremin 2017; Zembylas & Bekerman 2013; Zembylas 2018), critical peace education centers context and agency as a way to mitigate asymmetrical power relationships that are reified through totalizing discourses and practices. More specifically, critical peace education hones in on context-specific structural inequities to illuminate how localized experiences may shape perceptions of peace. In particular, it magnifies the role of critical pedagogy in this process, so that participants in peace education programs ostensibly have more room to foster a sense of transformative agency specific to their localized contexts (Bajaj 2008; Bajaj & Brantmeier 2011; Bajaj & Hantzopoulos 2016; Hantzopoulos 2011, 2016b). Critical peace education acknowledges not only the importance of local context but also how this local context engages with global phenomena like migration, climate change, racism, neoliberal economic policies that widen the gap between rich and poor, and regional and civil wars.

Moreover, scholars like Kurian (2020), Ragland (2018), Shirazi (2011), Williams (2016), Zakharia (2017), and Zembylas (2018) have pushed for placing postcolonial and decolonial theory in conversation with critical peace education efforts to understand how colonial legacies, both past and present, factor into how societies may conceptualize both peace and violence and the contributions of education therein. While this approach expands upon the emphasis on power—and its analysis—found in critical peace education, the postcolonial lens provides more fertile terrain for societies still grappling with the effects and realities of imperial and colonial violence to imagine more just futures specific to their histories and contexts. It also pushes scholars to consider how larger structural, material, and political realities serve to mediate contextually bound values that are prevalent in dominant peace research paradigms (Zakharia 2017).

These new generative directions have contributed greatly to the field. In addition to conceptualizing critical peace education (Bajaj 2008; Bajaj & Brantmeier 2011; Diaz-Soto 2005), its post-structural critiques (Gur–Ze'ev 2001; Hantzopoulos 2010; Kester & Cremin 2017; Zembylas & Bekerman 2013) and its postcolonial and decolonial forms (Shirazi 2011;

Williams 2013; Zakharia 2017; Zembylas 2018), peace education scholars have used these framings to engage in more empirical work with an eye toward these critical analyses. For example, Williams's (2013) ethnographic study of "violences" in schools in Trinidad and Tobago builds on Galtung's (1969) seminal ideas of direct, structural, and cultural violence by introducing the concept of discursive violence. In this analysis, youth emerge as the "main analytic unit in the discourse around school violence" while the structural role of class-stratified school systems—themselves vestiges of colonial governance—is often ignored. This focus on individual students instead of schools themselves, according to Williams (2013), is an exemplar of discursive violence and serves to preclude "neo-colonial structures, processes, and practices from substantive critique" (55). Further, Williams (2016) posits how these myopic understandings of school violence that focus on youth as perpetrators not only mask how adults actually perpetuate violence through their school-sanctioned interventions but also ultimately lead to ineffective approaches to violence reduction. Conversely, he notes that teachers' "nascent praxes of care" may be understood as forms of peace education (Williams 2017) in this context, an issue also addressed by Bermeo (2016b), who demonstrates how teachers negotiate their roles as agents of peace within the context of Ecuador's violent drug trade. Other scholars, like Chubbuck and Zembylas (2011), have also made significant contributions to the literature on school violence from a peace perspective, noting the ideological link between definitions of school violence and approaches toward nonviolence and peace education in schools.

Peace education scholarship has also demonstrated how violence—within the context of schooling—is varied and complex. For example, Hantzopoulos (2012a, 2016a, b) and Chubbuck and Zembylas (2011) write about the importance of care as a central form of peace education praxis in response to larger issues of structural violence facing youth in urban schools. According to these authors, these forms of violence range from degrading and humiliating school disciplinary policies, punitive high-stakes testing, narrow curricula, class size, and, frankly, broader, broader issues of structural racism and pervasive economic inequalities that frame the context in which students are going to school. Bickmore's (2011, 2014) study of bullying in schools also highlights how school violence is situated within a social context. The school and classroom environments, the community's shared ideas about bullying, and previous reactions to incidents of bullying contribute to the complexity of the problem. Given the link between definitions of school violence and approaches toward peace education, Bickmore's (2011) study suggests the need for 1) well-informed, critical, meta-analyses of violence in schools and 2) anti-violence initiatives that are comprehensive, long-range, and focused on developing new skills among students, administrators, and teachers. This growing body of scholarship has contributed to dynamic conceptual understandings of violence in schools and, within the context of teaching and learning, informing global efforts to end all forms of violence in schools (e.g., UNICEF 2018).

Moreover, peace education scholarship has demonstrated how schools and education can address contemporary direct, structural, and cultural violence in broader society by revealing the ways they maintain and uphold it. For example, Duckworth (2015) shows how US schools superficially and incompletely remember and teach about the attacks on the Twin Towers in NYC on September 11, 2001. She argues for more nuanced and historicized approaches, rather than merely commemorative ones, in order to build a critically engaged citizenry for peace. Similarly, Naseem and Arshad-Ayaz (2017) consider how education—both in schools and beyond—often serve to foster violent extremism through their hidden and narrow curricula. They consider how teachers and their pedagogies can disrupt these processes to foster inclusive and authentic participation and public discourse on issues related to extremism and radicalization.

Related to this, there is a significant body of peace education scholarship that examines how initiatives, programs, and approaches actively work to counter structural violence and provide robust examples of this in action. For example, Hantzopoulos (2011, 2013, 2016b) looks at critical peace education in public school settings and within the context urban school reform, providing concrete examples for the realization of whole-school approaches to peace education. Among other key themes, her research highlights the importance of building flattened relationships among students and between students and teachers; consideration of physical space in schools and its role in community building; and nonpunitive, alternative, and restorative approaches to discipline where multiple perspectives (including those of students) are welcome. Similarly, Brantmeier (2011) argues for the role that peace education plays in shaping teachers and their practice and, in particular, calls for schools of education to "openly embrace some of the broader and holistic purposes of education, such as the promotion of peace and social justice" (350). He provides keen insight into all the ways that peace education merges and should be a part of teacher education.

The field of peace education has also seen a proliferation of empirical and theoretical scholarship and research that has focused on education for peace and reconciliation in conflict-affected contexts (e.g., McGlynn, et al. 2009) and within global educational policy (e.g., Novelli & Smith 2011). These studies have encompassed vast types of programs across contexts and locations, including global and state-sponsored programs (e.g., Shah et al. 2016; Zakharia 2016), teaching and learning about competing and contested historical narratives (e.g., Bekerman & Zembylas 2011; Bellino 2017), youth encounter programs for young people from "conflict zones" (e.g., Ross 2017; Hantzopoulos 2010), integrated schooling in divided societies (e.g., Bekerman 2016; McGlynn 2009), and everyday school structures and programming in war-afflicted environments (e.g., Zakharia 2017).

As violence assumes many forms, examples of peace and peace education must be context-specific, multifaceted, and complex. Critical peace education has moved the field forward by pushing for continuous acknowledgment of the intricacies and nuances in studying and articulating peace and violence. Amplified by and intersecting with the discussions about postcolonial and post-structural theory, decolonization, and broader peace education (Hantzopoulos 2010; Kester & Cremin 2017; Ragland, 2018; Shirazi 2011; Williams 2016; Zakharia 2017; Zembylas 2018; Zembylas & Bekerman 2013), Bajaj and Hantzopoulos (2016) also point out that conventional approaches toward peace education do not always produce intended outcomes, despite good intentions. However, critical approaches have pushed the field to continually include critical reflection before, during, and after the implementation of peace education initiatives. As well, more empirical research is needed to help develop theory and explicate the practice of critical peace education that is particular to specific contexts.

More recently, there have been calls for "transrational perspectives" on peace education (Dietrich 2012, 2013, 2018; Echavarría Alvarez, Ingruber and Koppensteiner 2018), which resonate with the Innsbruck school's transrational approach to peace studies. According to Tjersland and Facci (2019), transrational approaches to peace education honor "the relationality and interconnectedness of educators, students, researchers and participants in all their human faculties. This includes to acknowledge and tap into not only the rational dimensions of being human, but also the emotional, mental and spiritual dimensions, in their complexity and in their ongoing and dynamic transformations" (248). Akin to cosmopolitanism (Appiah 2007a; Snauwaert 2008), which is grounded in universal experiences that connect and bind humanity, transrational approaches embrace the contextual to engage with other theories and lived realities of peace, education, and conflict; thus they embrace the fluidity of the "transrational," "as it changes and broadens, deepens and transforms in resonance with the contexts and relationships in place . . . entail[ing] a dialogue between different researchers and practitioners as regards to how the 'transrational,' in its varied shapes and expressions, is tapped into, understood, envisioned and engaged within multiple perspectives, approaches and processes of peace education" (248). Such approaches engage alongside and overlap with both the critical and decolonial approaches that are shaping the myriad trajectories of the field.

Conclusion

Overall, these distinct meanings of peace and peace education contribute to the diversity of perspectives and practices necessary for the field to move forward. Just like schools, nonformal and informal educational spaces can play host to peace teaching and learning because "peace education can happen anywhere" (Bajaj & Hantzopoulos 2016: 6). Additional directions in peace education speak to the rich range in definitions of peace and peace education, including a focus on the intersection with Indigenous scholarship and decolonization (Sumida-Huaman 2011), contemplative holistic and spiritual perspectives and practice (Lin, Oxford, & Brantmeier 2013), grassroots initiatives (Ross 2017), and the sociopolitics of multilingualism and language education (Bekerman 2016; Zakharia & Bishop 2013). While still evolving and transforming, recent calls for even more empirical studies (Bajaj & Hantzopoulos 2016) and evaluation (Del Felice, Karako, & Wisler 2015) will only strengthen the field with more robust theory and practice.

Given the realities that face our planet—climate change and (un)natural disasters; perpetual war and militarism, state-sanctioned and authoritarian violence in all corners of the globe; precarious migrations and increasing xenophobia and hate crimes across locales; global pandemics that expose differential vulnerabilities and impacts; stark and growing economic disparities; ongoing effects of colonialism and settler colonialism on Black, Indigenous and Native populations; and gender-based violence that continues to terrorize women and people who identify as LGBTQIA+[4] and gender-fluid—the varied directions and approaches to peace education attempt to reimagine and create more just and equitable futures. By highlighting these wide-ranging directions of the field, this chapter recognizes these debates about the multiple avenues to peace and justice, and that these trajectories are often personal, usually global, and always contextual.

2

Peace Education in Practice

Examples from the United States[1]

Chapter Outline

Critical Peace Education Theories and Practice: Situating
  Restorative Justice in the United States   36
The Truth Telling Project   39
Restorative Justice in NYC Schools   42
Conclusion   49

In this chapter, we illuminate the ways in which peace education might manifest in action and, in particular, respond to and engage with the rampant racism and structural violence that pervades all areas of life in the United States. From police violence, to increased incarceration rates, to egregious health disparities, to inadequate housing, to unequal and segregated educational opportunities and more, Black, Indigenous, and other people of color (BIPOC) communities in the United States have endured centuries of racist policies that not only are state-sanctioned and systemic but also make them more vulnerable to premature death (Gilmore 2007). Specifically, we explore more closely how approaches to restorative justice in the United States intersect with many of the theories, purposes, and goals of peace education, including in its critical and postcolonial (and dynamic) forms. Given the settler-colonial legacies and racialized violence that still remain unaddressed in the United States, this chapter considers how these justice-based initiatives, grounded in localized agency and transformation, might move communities, even partially, toward worlds more free of violence and closer to just visions of peace.

In particular, we shed light on two specific examples of context-driven restorative and transformative justice initiatives in practice. The first case study is a community-based approach that emerged from St. Louis and Ferguson, Missouri, called the Truth Telling Project (TTP). This initiative was born in the wake of the protests over the murder of an unarmed African American teenager, Michael Brown, in 2014 by the Ferguson police and endeavors to amplify community voices about structural violence and systemic racism through community-centered storytelling. Through this process, the TTP shares stories, facilitates healing, and supports on-the-ground activists in the pursuit of more just futures and structural transformation for vulnerable communities shaped by racial and state-sanctioned violence (Ragland 2015). The second case study broadly looks at school-based restorative approaches prevalent in New York City public schools that have proliferated in the last ten to fifteen years. While most New York City schools have yet to adopt these practices, there is a growing movement of schools and programs that is implementing these initiatives in order to create more humanized and dignified spaces for youth in schools (Hantzopoulos 2013, 2016a). We consider how these programs cultivate these spaces and also seek to interrupt the racialized, punitive and degrading practices that lead to phenomena like school push out and the school-to-prison pipeline. Specifically, we look at how restorative justice processes are undertaken at one particular school to provide a more fleshed-out account of how this approach might transform school culture and student experiences (Hantzopoulos 2013, 2016a).

Both of these initiatives draw on peace education explicitly or implicitly, and we locate them within peace education praxis accordingly. Together, these two cases and types of programs give the reader a small window into what organic and context-specific peace education initiatives might look like on the ground, whether in a community-based setting or in formal schooling contexts, to further understand peace education in practice.

Critical Peace Education Theories and Practice: Situating Restorative Justice in the United States

As discussed in Chapter 1, peace education is concerned with the abolition of all forms of violence, including direct and physical, structural, and cultural, in order to create more just and sustainable futures. Reardon (2001), as cited in Ragland (2018), defines violence as "avoidable, intentional harm, inflicted for a purpose or perceived advantage of the perpetrator or of those who, while not direct perpetrators, are, however, advantaged by the harm" (Reardon 2001: 35). While the definition is broad, it implicitly encompasses the differentiated forms of violence and grounds some of the theories that undergird peace education. Through the process of dismantling these forms of violence, peace education not only seeks to eliminate direct harm to attain "negative peace" but also seeks to eradicate structural and cultural violence so that "positive peace" flourishes. In fact, comprehensive peace cannot truly exist unless both negative peace and positive peace are realized.

While peace education more broadly considers the forms of structural violence that affect all communities across the globe, critical forms of peace education scholarship have pushed the field to grapple more deeply with the normative and Western-centric roots and research of the field (also explained more explicitly in Chapter 1, but briefly reviewed here as well). Often guided by postcolonial, decolonial, or post-structural lenses, theorists have urged more critical engagement with these colonialist roots to consider the ways broader peace education projects may reify asymmetries of power and forms of violence, in their seemingly benign attempts for resolution (Gur-Ze'ev 2001; Hantzopoulos 2010; Kester & Cremin 2017; Ragland 2015; Sumida-Huaman 2011; Tandon 1989; Zembylas & Bekerman 2013; Zembylas 2018).

In tandem with these theoretical considerations, other scholars have also urged for more empirical work that centers localized experiences so that the field complicates normative understandings of peace and violence as communities consider alternative futures and presents (Bajaj 2008; Bajaj & Brantmeier 2011; Brantmeier 2013; Diaz-Soto 2005). As a result, there has been a proliferation of empirical work in recent years that centers local meanings, often attending to the ways in which racism, context, and colonialism explicitly deepen our understandings of structural violence and produce more nuanced and varied definitions of peace (Bajaj 2015, 2016; Bajaj & Hantzopoulos 2016; Bekerman 2016; Bermeo 2016a; Hantzopoulos 2010, 2011b, 2016b; Murphy et al. 2016; Ragland 2015, 2018; Shirazi 2011; Williams 2016; Zakharia 2017; Zembylas 2016, 2018). The definitions of peace and embodiments of peace education practices that arise from these studies often depart or complicate the normative, liberal understandings that frame peace in a larger sense. While these situated definitions are often contradictory, paradoxical, and complex, they are more informative for particular communities seeking to dismantle violent structures because they are grounded in local contexts and meanings.[2]

With respect to the United States, some scholars have pushed for more localized and postcolonial readings when discussing violence and peace, particularly given the enduring legacies of racism, patriarchy, and settler-colonial violence. For example, Hantzopoulos (2016b) debunks the myth of "American exceptionalism" when it comes to peace education, which is often relegated to "conflict zones" in proximity to or within the Global South. She urges that US schools necessarily must embody a critical peace educational framework to engage the violent legacies of racist and settler-colonial histories and experiences that have framed, and continue to frame, the national (educational) project.

Similarly, Ragland (2018) deeply considers the role of a more critical and postcolonial peace education within the United States, given the prolonged and present realities that persist from the nation's colonialist and racist roots. Williams (2016) refers to such undercurrents as "lingering colonialities" that shape and contextualize violence and peace in postcolonial settings. As Ragland (2018) posits, these undercurrents also pervade the fields of peace education and conflict studies. He argues that, while these fields often address physical violence and structural violence, much of the scholarship fails to acknowledge coloniality and racism, particularly in "Western" or "Global North" contexts. This omission generates blind spots in analysis and development of the fields. For example:

> Our attempts to come to grips with this troubling, oppressive, violent past and to understand the ongoing racial injustice and suppression of subaltern voices are often pacified and given cursory attention in efforts to "move on," "unify and bring people together," "provide a solution," and even "make peace." Attempts at discourse meant to address structural violence in communities experiencing systemic injustices often amount to what Amartya Sen describes as "cultural violence": marginalizing local voices in communities, imposing solutions to "fix" them. (Ragland 2018: 524)

In other words, as many of the previously mentioned theorists articulate, the peace education project potentially goes awry when (1) there is sole reliance on Western-centric normative notions of peace, (2) there is a failure to acknowledge the sui generis contexts (including the ways in which race and coloniality inform local practices) under which violence occurs, and (3) marginalized voices are dismissed in the need for a teleological outcome that does not often benefit them or improve their lives. In the context of the United States, these points equally and just as urgently apply.

Critical, postcolonial, and decolonizing forms and approaches of peace education open up space for new realities and imaginaries when marginalized communities are centered as the drivers of resistance, justice, peace, and change. While there are myriad examples of such initiatives in the larger context of the United States,[3] we focus on two dialogical and restorative justice spaces—the Truth Telling Project, which began in Missouri, and restorative justice efforts in New York schools—to show how these critical forms of peace education transpire in action. Since each case is context-specific, the descriptions of the embodiments provided in the following paragraphs help define and shape how these restorative practices might function as conduits to not only disrupt racist practices but also shape new more liberatory futures.

The Truth Telling Project

In 2014 and 2015, US cities like Baltimore, Maryland; Ferguson, Missouri; and other urban centers erupted in uprisings and protests against racialized police violence and brutality. While state-sanctioned racial violence has existed in the United States since the nation's founding, the murders of unarmed Black men such as Michael Brown in Ferguson (2014), Eric Garner in New York (2014), and Freddie Gray in Baltimore (2015), and the subsequent unaccountability of the police officers who killed them, catalyzed a movement that brought structural racism, past and present, to the forefront. Moreover, this flashpoint occurred in tandem with the news that George Zimmerman, the person who killed Trayvon Martin, an unarmed Black teenager, was acquitted of all charges. In response, Alicia Garza, Patrisse Cullors, and Opal Tometi launched the viral hashtag #BlackLivesMatter (BLM), giving rise to broader coalitions like the Movement for Black Lives. According to Ragland (2018):

> Given the legacy of injustice that characterizes US dealings with Black folk, intergenerational harm, trauma, and structural and direct violence continue to teach marginalized communities about the value of their lives. These teachings simultaneously induce silence and continued violence because of the intransigence of racism and white supremacy in many institutions and policies that deal with marginalized communities. In the United States, Ferguson became the flashpoint in confronting the racist past that reverberates throughout of American life. (520)

As well, the continued police and state-sanctioned violence and murders against unarmed Black people—including children like Tamir Rice or the mysterious "suicide" of Sandra Bland while in police custody, or most recently, the killings of George Floyd, Breonna Taylor, Elijah McClain, and Tony McDade—has prompted the rest of the world to recognize that this phenomenon is deeply systemic in the United States. Some countries, like the Bahamas, issued travel warnings for their citizens (the majority of whom are of African descent), stating "The Ministry of Foreign Affairs and Immigration has taken a note of the recent tensions in some American cities over shootings of young Black males by police officers . . . In particular young males are asked to exercise extreme caution in affected cities in their interactions with the police. Do not be confrontational and cooperate" (Ministry of Foreign Affairs, Government of Bahamas 2016). Amnesty International (2015a) published an extensive report, *Deadly Force: Police Use of Lethal Force in the United States*, documenting the widespread pattern of racial discrimination and lethal police violence mostly toward Black men, but also Black women, and Latinx and Indigenous communities. Their thorough report shows both how the numbers are underreported and how the use of lethal force by law enforcement officers "raises serious human rights concerns, including in regard to the right to life, the right to security of the person, the right to freedom from discrimination and the right to equal protection of the law" (Amnesty International 2015a: 1).

The Truth Telling Project of Ferguson thus emerged out of this context of heightened awareness and coverage of the enduring state violence toward Black people in the United States. According to Ragland (2018), it emerged contextually and from a grassroots base "as a community initiative and educational intervention, rooted in restorative and transformative justice, to challenge narratives that justify harm leveled against Black people, while building community efficacy through the telling of stories that reflect the experience of those most victimized by direct and structural violence" (521). In particular, the TTP embraces storytelling as a form of resilience and dissent, centers marginalized narratives, places truth at the foreground, and considers intergenerational trauma and struggle as part of the process of transformation and resistance.

At the heart of the work are narratives and stories, framed by shared experiences of racial violence (structural, direct, and cultural) that are deeply rooted in the fabric of the United States. According to Romano and Ragland (2018), these counternarratives, much like in the tradition of critical race theory, not only interrupt dominant narratives that circulate but also serve as a form of collective and community agency. Moreover, the TTP distinguishes itself from the more known Truth and Reconciliation Processes, as the latter seek resolution and/or reconciliation as an ostensible goal. Instead, the TTP welcomes ambiguity and views truthtelling as a form of healing, albeit nonteleological and linear, shaped explicitly by the communities most affected by the injustices. Table 2.1 reflects the current goals, mission, and strategy of the TTP to articulate this vision.

Central to the TTP's work is the aspect of healing, storytelling, and agency for the most marginalized, but the TTP also includes an educational arm so that adult and high school age educators, dialogue facilitators, and learners, as well as white allies, have a platform to consider how to act for racial justice. The primary purpose of this platform, known as the Truth Telling Commons,

Table 2.1 Current Mission, Goals, and Strategy of TTP

Mission: The Truth Telling Project implements and sustains grassroots, community-centered truth-telling processes to amplify our voices about police violence and its roots. We foster coalition-building and solidarity with the most vulnerable communities. We educate ourselves and our allies about systemic violence throughout the United States. We support reparative and restorative justice as the primary pathways for structural transformation.

Goal: The Truth Telling Project seeks to engage the U.S. in stories that galvanize thoughtful, empathetic and educated allies for Black and communities of color. By encouraging "witnesses" to listen to and reflect on voices "from the margins," our hope is that more individuals and communities might become interested in ending the structural and militarized violence in the U.S. We work to help people understand the deep seated institutional racism that allows for police violence to occur, and the pervasive impact that violence has on families and their communities. We ultimately encourage empathy and anti-racist learning among ally communities, and lead people to The Movement for Black Lives and other racial justice organizations as supporters.

Strategy: Testimony that exposes the experiences of people and communities that suffer from state sanctioned violence:

Internal education within the organization and external education within communities

Healing within communities that experience police violence with the hope for broader reconciliation

Supportive networks for families dealing with police and state sanctioned violence

Solidarity among and between allies, organizers and educators to engage their community around issues of racial justice to encourage P.O.C-led [people of color] action

Collaboration with individuals and groups with related struggles

Embodiment of our values, such as democratic womanism, queer affirmative, de-colonialism, and anti-racist values in our personal and professional practices.

Sourced from TTP's website, www.truthtellingproject.org

is to house testimony from the Ferguson Truth Telling Hearings; however, this educational outreach is also a core focus of working toward racial justice, sharing stories widely per the wishes of community members telling them. By using this online platform, this initiative creates meaningful dialogical spaces for white and other non-Black folks to deeply listen, so that they can reflect on how to take action in response to state-sanctioned violence, without further burdening those that have been harmed by anti-Black racial injustice. Ragland (2018) explains how this might transpire in the following passage:

> the Truth Telling Commons . . . document[s] inequity by bridging what is often a gap between data on racial injustices and empathic connections needed to act against racially charged direct and indirect violence enacted on people of color. We also hope it will foster political efficacy in communities through extending marginalized, authentic voices to educate and break through racial stereotypes, apathy, and inaction. Through sharing the experiences of Black communities and our experiences with police violence, the online learning platform…is rooted in a community of healing and support, as it develops political strength. It seeks to foster and disseminate stories and testimonies, engaging with the local and national community of human rights and racial justice . . . it also connects partner organizations by guiding users to issues that emerge from testimonies to become active with groups working on those same issues. The stories fill in the gaps for national and global audiences as they witness an empowered community that shares its testimony and informs the world of how their stories bring clarity to the larger landscape of police violence with structural racism at its core. Our stories illustrate the specificity of human dignity and this platform and its dissemination will connect learners to this orientation to inform their work. (532)

As Ragland points out, the aims of the TTP and its various strategies embody many of the aspects of critical forms of peace education, including centering coloniality, race, and localized contexts to engender more particular, emergent, and ground-up approaches to collective agency, transformation, and deep social change. Moreover, as will be discussed in Chapter 5, the emphasis on agency and dignity—in this initiative, but also in general—bridges this form of critical peace education with transformative forms of human rights education as well.

Restorative Justice in NYC Schools

In the last fifteen years, there has also been an incremental rise of restorative justice initiatives in schools across the United States broadly and in New

York City (NYC) specifically, which exemplify a form of peace education in practice. These programs, which focus on repair, healing, community, and transformation, are often seen as an alternative to the punitive disciplinary policies that rapidly proliferated, took hold, and still persist in most cases in NYC schools over the last several decades (Foster 2015; Gregory et al. 2016; Hantzopoulos 2011a, 2013; Jensen 2015; Kelvan 2018; Manassah, Roderick, & Gregory 2018; Marsh 2017; Sandwick, Hahn, & Ayoub 2019). While explained in more detail further in this section, these initiatives aim to center voice, agency, dignity, and humanity in their approaches to both dealing with community harm and community building (Hantzopoulos 2011a, 2013, 2016a; Gregory et al. 2016; Manassah, Roderick, & Gregory 2018; Marsh 2017; Sandwick, Hahn, & Ayoub 2019; Wadwha 2015).

Like the Truth Telling Project, such initiatives in NYC schools are born out of the harmful, retributory, and violent measures that are often reproduced in school settings. For instance, many studies reveal the disproportionate ways that zero-tolerance strategies subject students to degrading treatment in the classroom, unfair disciplinary measures and outcomes, and threatening police and security presence in schools, and ultimately contribute to hostile learning environments that punish students severely for minor infractions (ACLU 2010; Boccanfusco & Kuhfeld 2011; Kreuger 2010; Lee et al. 2011; Morris 2005; New York Civil Liberties Union Make the Road, & Annenberg Institute of School Reform 2009; Suh & Suh 2007; Sullivan 2007; Vincent, Sprague, & Tobin 2012; Welch & Payne 2011). Because of this empirical link among excessively punitive disciplinary policies, corresponding high suspension rates, and ultimately, higher dropout rates (see Christie, Jolivette, & Nelson 2007; Suh & Suh 2007), many scholars and youth advocates prefer the term "push out" to describe the phenomenon of students leaving school (NYCLU 2009; Sullivan 2007). Moreover, there is also substantial research and evidence that shows in the long term, high school dropout rates are related to increased involvement in the juvenile justice system (Morris & Perry 2016; Skiba, Arrendondo, & Williams 2014), often referred to as the school-to-prison pipeline (Meiners & Winn 2010).

This phenomenon of harsh and exclusionary discipline is deeply racialized in the United States. For instance, many scholars have documented the ways in which students, particularly those who are Black, Indigenous, and other People of Color (BIPOC), are often framed and criminalized in their school environments and constructed as "trouble," and are thereby disproportionately and egregiously impacted by these policies (Annamma, Morrison, & Jackson 2014; Fenning & Rose 2007; Ferguson 2001; Morris 2005; Mazama & Lundy 2012; Skiba,

Arredondo, &Williams 2014; Tuck 2012; Vincent, Sprague, & Tobin 2012; Wilson, Yull, & Massey 2020). Moreover, despite many studies focusing on the impact on boys, recent studies show that impacts of such policies are just as severe, particularly on Black girls (Crenshaw, Priscilla, & Jyoti 2015; Morris 2016), who are often subjected to adultification bias (Epstein, Blake, and Gonzalez, 2017), and those with disabilities (Annamma, Morrison, & Jackson 2014). Some egregious cases, highlighted in the media, include the handcuffed arrest of a twelve-year-old girl in Queens for doodling on a desk (Monahan 2010). Another recent incident involves a six-year-old girl who was handcuffed, arrested, and taken to a juvenile center for merely not wanting to engage and crying at school—ostensibly typical behavior for any child that age (Padilla 2019). As most of the globe moved schooling remote in 2020 with the rise of Covid-19, examples emerged such as that of a teacher calling the police to go to the home of a Black seventh-grade student in Colorado and, subsequently, suspending the student for having a foam toy gun toy appear in the video screen of his online class (Peiser 2020). While these may seem like extreme examples, the aforementioned reports and studies above confirm that this type of humiliating, degrading, and ultimately harmful treatment is all too commonplace in schools that serve BIPOC youth.[4]

Despite claims that such "no excuses" approaches create safer schools, these punitive measures instead create hostile learning environments, ones that often mirror prison-like systems of law and order that some have coined the "school-prison nexus" (Krueger 2010). As already mentioned, students who are frequently disciplined or suspended from school are much more likely to not complete high school. In part, this is because such exclusionary and harsh discipline policies often work in tandem with high-stakes testing; the former criminalizes students for minor infractions of school rules, and the latter forces administrators to push out low-performing students to improve their school's overall test scores (Advancement Project et al. 2011; American Civil Liberties Union 2010). While research also shows that individual, social, cultural, psychological, and economic variables may also contribute to dropout patterns (Rumberger 2004), the studies articulate the importance of school culture on the retention and attainment rate of students in school. Tuck's (2012) work captures how such structures create "humiliating ironies" for students that propel their disengagement, and eventual departure, from school. In other words, punitive policies—with regard to behavior, academics, and testing—work together to make schools antagonistic spaces for many youth.

In response to these demoralized environments, scholars and organizations have urged schools to adopt more humane frameworks in their approaches. This framework should include "not only teaching essential academic knowledge and skills, but also creating a positive school environment, supporting the emotional and behavioral development of young people, and encouraging students to participate in developing school policies that impact their education" (Sullivan 2007: 45). Many studies empirically validate this approach, revealing how strong student-teacher relationships, positive and caring school cultures, and student-centered and culturally-relevant academic curricula can reduce dropout rates and diminish inequities in schooling (Antrop-Gonzalez 2011; de Jesús 2012; Hantzopoulos 2011b, 2012a, b, 2016a; Rivera-McCutchen 2012; Rodriguez & Conchas 2008; Tyner-Mullings 2015).

Restorative practices in schools are often at the heart of such environments (Hantzopoulos 2016a). For instance, Manassah, Roderick, and Gregory (2018) explain how restorative practices strengthen social emotional learning, relationships, and community in a school environment to build more positive school cultures. Hantzopoulos (2016a) demonstrates how cultures of care, respect, participation, and critical questioning in schools are supported by integrated restorative practices (and other practices); in turn, these vital components make up the fabric of what it takes to create dignified and humane schools for youth in which they can thrive and flourish. As Foster (2015) explains, restorative approaches center the lived experiences of students which then help disrupt harmful disciplinary policies. Schools with restorative approaches have noted dramatic *decreases* in behavioral incidents and disciplinary sanctions (both in-school measures and out-of-school suspensions) since implementation (Community Asset Development Redefining Education [CADRE] 2010; Lewis 2009).

While there has also been an incremental rise in restorative practices nationwide, New York City in particular has seen a rise in practices over the last ten years (see Ancess et al. 2019; Davidson 2014; Foster 2015; Gregory et al. 2016; Hantzopoulos 2011a, 2013, 2016a; Klevan 2018; Lustick 2017; Manassah, Roderick, & Gregory 2018; Marsh 2017; Sandwick, Hahn, & Ayoub 2019; Wadwha 2015, for case studies). This is in part because paradoxically, in the late mid-to-late 1990s, zero-tolerance policies and police presence in NYC public schools were also (and continue to be) normalized in school settings. In response, progressive educators, advocates, and students were actively seeking alternatives to counter these trends. Groups like the New York Collective of Radical Educators, Teachers Unite, and the National Economic and Social Rights Initiative (NESRI) organized workshops, roundtables, and discussions on restorative practices in schools. According to Teachers Unite (A. Bean 2015, personal communication), an informal poll garnered from their trainings show that more than seventy-five public middle and high schools in the city have incorporated some sort of restorative disciplinary practices, and roughly twenty-five schools have integrated restorative practices more fully and comprehensively (Hantzopoulos 2016a: 165–6).

Thus, while many schools embody and have embraced these practices, we focus on one school, Humanities Preparatory Academy (Prep), a small New York City public high school that uses a restorative justice model called the Fairness Committee (Fairness) to illustrate one such approach. The James Baldwin School, which shares the same mission and vision as Prep and is colocated in the same building, also adopts this model. Moreover, while other New York City schools are starting to adopt restorative justice models, Prep pioneered this approach by having the Fairness Committee in place since the school's inception in 1996. It therefore has a solid, decades-long record of this enduring practice. In fact, on their website, they share that "Every school in New York City currently practicing restorative justice was at some point trained by Humanities Prep staff and students" (https://humanitiesprep.org/restorative-justice-and-fairness).

Research drawing on data from the school shows that most students believe the school creates a humane environment in which a culture of respect, tolerance, and democracy flourishes, crystallized in restorative structures like Fairness. It is often in these spaces that students can influence and implement school-wide policy through an emphasis on critical dialogue and direct model of community action. Many students feel the Fairness Committee positively contributes to a safe environment and helps them grow personally, and they also view it is a fundamental mechanism to build community and forge stronger relationships among student peers and teachers. As a result, many students, including those who had previously felt marginalized from schooling, find refuge and acceptance at this school and are able to succeed and thrive academically (Hantzopoulos 2013, 2016a).

The school itself was originally created not only to reengage students that were potentially at-risk for dropping out but also to help prepare them for life beyond graduation, including college. While the school presently serves a mixed population of students who have succeeded in other schools and those who have struggled, it continues to attempt to reach all students "by personalizing our learning situations, by democratizing and humanizing the school environment, and by creating a 'talking culture,' an atmosphere of informal intellectual discourse among students and faculty" (Humanities Preparatory Academy n.d: 2). Grounded in the school's core values of respect for humanity, diversity, truth, and the intellect and commitment to democracy, peace, and justice, Prep endeavors to provide a transformative schooling experience for those who come through its doors. It remains rather small for a New York City high school (currently at around 250), though it shares space with many other schools in a larger educational facility. The school's demographic composition reflects the racial and economic spectrum of New York City.[5]

Fairness is a mechanism through which students can discuss with one another, and with teachers, violations of the community's core values and brainstorm alternatives and solutions to these dilemmas. Students and teachers can take other students to Fairness, and students are even able to take teachers, though this happens less frequently. Examples where a student or teacher might be taken to Fairness are wide-ranging and include inappropriate language, missing class, questions over grading, hurtful speech, vandalism, and the silencing of other community members. When a committee is convened, students and teachers are encouraged to ask questions, listen to all parties, and help uncover what transpired. The structure strives to emphasize process and real dialogue over product and fixed outcome, so the end result is sui generis to each particular committee meeting (Hantzopoulos 2011a). It operates much like a rotating reparative committee that involves all members of the school community, including students, teachers, and office staff. Minimally, the committee hearing the "cases" should have two students and one teacher, as well as a teacher facilitator. Because the aim is to include all school-community members in the process, the committee is not fixed and is put together on a case-by-case basis, drawing on the pool of the school population (much like how juries in the United States are comprised) (Hantzopoulos 2013, 2106a). Table 2.2 excerpts how the school describes the purpose and structure of the committee.

While the structure of Fairness continues to morph and evolve over time, it is essentially designed for members of the community to grapple with the broader core values of the school when infractions arise among them. Yet, Fairness extends beyond consequences and reparations; it also contributes to generating a positive school environment. For instance, since grievances must be framed in relationship to one of the core values as mentioned earlier, Fairness also builds positive school culture by supporting the diffusion of the

Table 2.2 Humanities Preparatory Academy Fairness Committee

The Fairness Committee of Humanities Preparatory Academy is a non-traditional restorative justice model of school discipline. Parameters and protocols for discussion place emphasis on the violation of community core norms and values rather than on the breaking of rules. Fairness seeks to create, through dialogue and by consensus, appropriate "consequences" for those violations, rather than simply mete out prescribed "punishments."

As a model of restorative justice the Committee endeavors to 1) inspire empathetic and critical self-reflection, by confronting a member of the community with his or her actions and how they have affected others; 2) collectively determine how best to restore and mend the community in the wake of actions inconsistent with its values; and 3) how to reintegrate the member of the community who has violated our values back into the fabric and culture of the school.

The Fairness Committee is a democratization of the traditional disciplinary process and includes all teachers and students. It typically convenes six people: one teacher facilitator, a teacher and two student committee members, and the two people who are involved in the norm/value violation. Any member of the community—teacher or student—can take another to Fairness.

The committee is convened ad hoc but regularly throughout the semester and facilitators reach out to new and veteran students and staff for inclusion on the committee. The entire school, with students at the center, is thus involved in the process of creating, through dialogue and by consensus, consequences for the violation of school-community norms.

Fairness Structure:

Roles: Facilitator; Panel: Two students, one teacher; Person taken to Fairness; Person bringing one to Fairness

The facilitator convenes the Fairness by introducing everyone and explaining the basic ground rules, which include confidentiality and openness to process. S/he also explains the way that the process works, including the speaking order and role of the panel. The person calling the Fairness is allowed to explain, uninterrupted, why s/he is doing it. S/he is asked to explain which core value s/he believes has been violated. Next, the person brought to Fairness explains his or her side of the story, also uninterrupted.

After that, the panel is allowed to ask questions to either person to obtain a more complete and holistic picture of the situation at hand. This process has no beginning or end and is dependent on the context of the situation and the nature of the dialogue. The intent is to come to some agreement or understanding among all parties. At times, this happens easily and other times requires much more work.

Sourced from Coalition of Essential Schools ChangeLab, as cited in Hantzopoulos 2008, p. 371

core values in the school, including furthering a democratizing and inclusive space as the composition of the committee draws from the entire school community, and anyone can be "taken" to the committee, including teachers and administrators. Moreover, students and alumni echoed these intents, repeatedly praising it and remarking that not only was it a structure that was unique in dealing with community concerns but also one that cultivated voice, allowed for questioning, and reinforced a caring community (see Hantzopoulos 2011a, 2013, and 2016a for more descriptive data about student and staff responses). This case description therefore provides insight into the ways that Fairness operates on the school level as one of many structures that encourages student voice, agency, and democratic participation to create a humanizing and dignified environment for young people.

Conclusion

This chapter dove into two examples of community- and school-based restorative justice praxis that brings the concepts of peace education to life in very distinct contexts. Both the Truth Telling Project and the Fairness Committee at Humanities Prep represent ways that critical and homegrown forms of peace education take shape in practice. Moreover, they both respond organically and specifically to forms of structural and cultural violence that not only permeate communities, systems, and schools but also are rooted in the racialized and settler-colonial legacies and realities of the United States. Both examples also rely on their organic, local, and internal processes to forge new ways of making meaning and reimagining the world. In the spirit of praxis, these forms of peace education are tweaked and continue to be remade given the shifting needs and circumstances of the communities involved. Such examples speak back to the normative imposition of peace education values from above and, instead, offer models of how "subjugated knowledges" from below can inform a more decolonial approach to peace education practice.

As we put the finishing touches on this manuscript, we see some of the widespread results of these ongoing and long-standing local initiatives as police brutality is once again in the national and international spotlight. These protests have spread across the globe, with people across continents standing up to the incessant harm and violence that has been leveled against

Black communities for centuries. In the United States, the Movement for Black Lives has made central a list of demands, including ones to redirect police funding and to remove police from schools. Many districts such as Oakland, California, and Minneapolis, Minnesota, have subsequently voted to remove police from schools as a result. These abolitionist demands are now being mainstreamed in public discourse and are the results of activists and educators, like the ones that we have just read about, who have been engaged in the struggle for years. By centering the experiences and stories of those that are often most affected by these forms of violence, these two examples show how agency and dignity are paramount to the process and efforts of peace education, and while sometimes these local efforts may seem small, they can be part of broader efforts and have larger effect. The next chapter, Chapter 3, turns to the intertwined field of human rights education (HRE) to explore its roots and manifestations, and we provide case studies of HRE practice in Chapter 4. We then revisit these themes of agency and dignity in Chapter 5 to examine the intersections of the two fields more closely.

Human Rights Education

Foundations, Frameworks, and Future Directions[1]

Chapter Outline

History, Models, and Institutionalization	52
Conceptual Orientations	62
Global Scholarship About HRE in Practice	63
Conclusion	77

Human rights education (HRE)—a field that utilizes teaching and learning processes in classrooms and communities to educate *about* basic rights and *for* the broadening of respect for the dignity and freedom of all people(s)— has expanded over the last several decades. Overall, its proliferation has been more practically and explicitly integrated into educational agendas and programs than peace education, yielding in many ways more robust and documented empirical scholarship than the former (even though peace education is likely happening in reality just as frequently). Since the founding of the United Nations (UN) and the adoption of the Universal Declaration of Human Rights (1948) after the Second World War, HRE has been held out as an ideal to ensure that institutions of formal learning (such as schools, colleges, and universities) become sites of promise and equity rather than breeding grounds for hate and violence. HRE has also been widely utilized in nonformal education settings, such as in museums and community-based organizations. Similar to the field of peace education, HRE emerged from the global energy that led to the creation of the UN and as a retort to the "direct" and "structural" violence (Galtung 1969) that led to 80 million deaths during Second World War (National Second World War Museum, n.d.). The trajectory of peace education and human rights education, however, has been distinct with the fields' own advocates and bodies of scholarship, despite their many linkages and overlapping priorities. In this chapter, we offer an overview of HRE's history, models, and conceptual underpinnings as presented through scholarship in the field.

History, Models, and Institutionalization

History

There have been many antecedents to human rights education in individual initiatives and social movements over centuries past. The modern field of human rights education, however, traces its origins back to the Universal Declaration of Human Rights (UDHR), adopted by the United Nations General Assembly in 1948. Soon after member states signed on to the United Nations Charter that established the organization in San Francisco in 1945, the United Nations established the UN Commission on Human Rights, a committee chaired by Eleanor Roosevelt (who by then was former first lady of the United States), to draft a Universal Declaration of Human Rights. Contributing to the drafting of the document were scholars and philosophers from Canada, France, Australia, China, Lebanon, India, Denmark, the Dominican Republic, the United Kingdom, the Soviet Union, Chile, and elsewhere. Many debates ensued over the period of the UDHR's drafting—including about individual versus collective rights; contestation over political, civic, economic, social, and cultural rights; the nature of rights and their enforcement; and how to ensure universal rights when many of the United Nations' founding members were still colonialists engaged in brutal repression in territories under their jurisdiction (Burke 2013).

In drafting Article 26 on education, the committee was compelled by arguments about going beyond the right to educational access. They wanted to move toward a more intentional purpose as had been argued for by the representative from the Jewish World Congress:

> Education in Germany and other fascist countries had been carried out in compliance with the principle of the right of education for everyone; yet the

doctrines on which that education had been founded had led to two world wars. If the Declaration failed to define the spirit in which future generations were to be educated, it would lose its value as a guide for humanity. It was necessary to stress the importance of the article devoted to the spirit of education, which was possibly greater than that of all the other articles of the Declaration. (Morsink 1999: 326)

Those involved in discussions of the Declaration—especially those who had seen the horrors of fascism, war, and genocide firsthand—highlighted that education had the potential to be directed toward peace and human rights, on the one hand, and toward indoctrination, brutality, and violence, on the other. As a result, part II of Article 26 was added, asserting the right not only to an education as indicated in part I but also to one directed toward "the full development of the human personality and to the strengthening of respect for human rights and fundamental freedoms" (UDHR 1948). The anchor for the field of human rights education comes from this part of Article 26, which enshrines a right to human rights education.

Despite its mention in the UDHR adopted by the UN General Assembly on December 10, 1948 (now commemorated annually as International Human Rights Day), human rights education as a global movement only gained significant momentum after the end of the Cold War in the early 1990s as it seemed a collective opportune moment with renewed global connection. The 1993 United Nations World Conference on Human Rights in Vienna was a watershed moment for HRE. The Vienna Declaration stated that "human rights education, training, and public information is essential for the promotion and achievement of stable and harmonious relations among communities and for fostering mutual understanding, tolerance, and peace" (United Nations 1993). The Vienna Declaration and Program of Action resulting from the Conference had an extensive subsection on human rights education and called for a United Nations Decade for Human Rights Education, which subsequently ensued from 1995 to 2004; the Decade brought policymakers, government officials, activists, and educators into more sustained conversation around HRE. As the UN Decade came to a close, the ongoing UN World Programme for Human Rights Education was established in 2005 and housed within the United Nations Office of the High Commissioner for Human Rights (OHCHR) in Geneva. In 2011, the UN General Assembly adopted the UN Declaration on Human Rights Education and Training (UNDHRET), further highlighting the importance of HRE at the level of national policy and reform. The backing of HRE by such high-profile global institutions has helped with its proliferation and acceptance worldwide.

Definitions and Models

While there are many approaches to human rights education, there is broad agreement about certain core components. First, most scholars and practitioners agree that HRE must include both *content* and *processes* related to teaching human rights (Flowers 2003; Meintjes 1997; Tibbitts 2002). Second, most literature in the field discusses the need for HRE to include goals related to cognitive (content), attitudinal or emotive (values/skills), and action-oriented components (Tibbitts 2005). Amnesty International's Human Rights Friendly Schools framework weaves together the intended outcomes of HRE by highlighting three prepositions linking education and human rights in a comprehensive manner: education *about* human rights (cognitive), education *through* human rights (participatory methods that create skills for active citizenship), and education *for* human rights (fostering learners' ability to speak out and act in the face of injustices) (as cited in Bajaj 2012).

Human rights education also has varied definitions depending on the proponent's ideology, social location, and approach. As defined by the United Nations (1998):

> Human rights education can be defined as education, training and information aiming at building a universal culture of human rights through the sharing of knowledge, imparting of skills and molding of attitudes directed to:
>
> (a) The strengthening of respect for human rights and fundamental freedoms;
> (b) The full development of the human personality and the sense of its dignity;
> (c) The promotion of understanding, tolerance, gender equality, and friendship among all nations, Indigenous peoples and racial, national, ethnic, religious, and linguistic groups;
> (d) The enabling of all persons to participate effectively in a free and democratic society governed by the rule of law;
> (e) The building and maintenance of peace;
> (f) The promotion of people-centered sustainable development and social justice. (UN 1998)

Knowledge about human rights and tolerance/acceptance of others is emphasized in the UN definition of HRE. UN initiatives are largely directed toward member states and attempt to foster adoption of national plans of action for integrating HRE into their educational systems.

Nongovernmental organizations (NGOs) and community-based organizations have also long been active in human rights education and utilize human rights discourse as a strategy to frame the demands of diverse social movements—a more ground-up approach to HRE. At the grassroots level, HRE has often taken the form of popular education or community education to mobilize constituencies for expanding social movements (Kapoor 2004). In Latin America, for example, many efforts aimed at HRE blossomed immediately after the end of dictatorships when NGOs that had fought for human rights turned their attention to education as a tool for reconciliation, justice, and the prevention of a return to authoritarian rule (Magendzo 1997). As such, human rights education efforts are seen as both a political and pedagogical strategy to facilitate democratization and active citizenship.

For definitional purposes, human rights education can take a variety of forms. In formal schooling, human rights can be integrated into textbooks or other subjects such as civics or social studies. In some places, direct instruction in a "human rights" class is mandated or offered as an elective in public or private schooling at the secondary level. In universities, undergraduate and graduate programs in "human rights" and increasingly in "human rights education" are emerging and becoming institutionalized. More commonly, optional programs exist either during the school day, after-school (through clubs or cocurricular programs), or through summer camps and other programs—all of which offer students exposure to human rights (as is true of peace education as well). In professional settings across the globe, human rights training—either optional or required, and ad-hoc or sustained—has been offered for judges, police officers, military personnel, health workers, and teachers, among others. Additionally, nonformal HRE is flourishing in community-based settings worldwide. Regardless of setting or form, the types of rights brought into focus (civil, political, social, economic, cultural, or a cross-section of equality rights for a specific group) depend on the context and the approach (see Table 3.1, developed by Nancy Flowers). Thus, human rights education varies in content, approach, scope, intensity, depth, and availability (Bajaj 2012).

Drawing on the promise of grassroots-level efforts to influence awareness about human rights, Amnesty International defines human rights education as the following:

> Human rights education is a deliberate, participatory practice aimed at empowering individuals, groups, and communities through fostering knowledge, skills, and attitudes consistent with internationally recognized principles . . . Its goal is to build a culture of respect for and action in the defense and promotion of human rights for all. (Amnesty International 2015b)

Table 3.1 Developmental and Conceptual Framework for Human Rights Education

Levels	Goals	Key Concepts	Practices	Specific Human Rights Problems	Education Standards & Instruments
Early Childhood * Preschool & lower Primary school * Ages 3 to 7	* Respect for self * Respect for parents and teachers * Respect for others	* Self * Community * Responsibility	* Fairness * Self-expression * Listening	* Racism * Sexism * Unfairness * Hurting people (emotionally or physically)	* Classroom rules * Family life * Community standards * Convention on the Rights of the Child (UNCRC)
Later Childhood * Upper primary school * Ages 8 to 11	* Social Responsibility * Citizenship * Distinguishing wants from needs from rights	* Individual rights * Group rights * Freedom * Equality * Justice * Rule of law * Government * Security * Democracy	* Valuing diversity * Fairness * Distinguishing between fact and opinion * Performing school and community service * Civic participation	* Discrimination/ prejudice * Poverty/hunger * Injustice * Ethnocentrism * Passivity	* UDHR * History of human rights * Local, national legal system * Local and national history in human rights terms * UNESCO, UNICEF

Adolescence * Lower secondary school * Ages 12 to 14	* Knowledge of specific human rights	* International law * World peace * World development * World political economy * World ecology * Legal rights * Moral rights	* Understanding other points of view * Citing evidence in support of ideas * Doing research/gathering information * Sharing information * Community service and action	* Ignorance * Apathy * Cynicism * Political repression * Colonialism/imperialism * Economic globalization * Environmental degradation	* UN Covenants * Elimination of racism * Elimination of sexism * Regional human rights conventions * NGOs
Older Adolescents and Adults * Upper secondary school and adult groups * Ages 15 and up	* Knowledge of human rights standards * Integration of human rights into personal awareness and behaviors	* Moral responsibility/literacy	* Participation in civic organizations * Fulfilling civic responsibilities * Civic disobedience * Community services and action	* Genocide * Torture	* Geneva Conventions * Specialized conventions * Evolving human rights standards

Adapted from the United Nations Document, *Guidelines for National Plans of Action for Human Rights Education. Developmental and Conceptual Framework for Human Rights Education* (Flowers 2003).

The Amnesty International definition places greater responsibility on human rights learners becoming activists for human rights through the process of HRE by sharing information with others and actively working to defend human rights. Thus, central to this definition are the outcome of social change and the agency of learners to claim their own rights and defend the rights of others. This approach to HRE accounts for some of the differences in the way individuals or organizations conceptualize it as an education reform or strategy.

As is the case with any field in development and in motion, there are many articulations of HRE models and approaches that emerge to understand and chart the boundaries of the field. Within the broad parameters of convergence discussed earlier, some differences in approaches and definitions have been put forth to further explore human rights education depending on what dimension is of most interest to the respective scholar. More recent articulations have elaborated the definition of what HRE must include in different contexts—beyond the teaching of international human rights norms and standards—and have cited a variety of goals and learners.

HRE models provide productive schemas for theorizing its emergence, conceptualization, and implementation across the globe. One vital forum is the online list-serve (now called a Global Community of Practice) and epistemic community coordinated by the US-based Human Rights Education Associates (HREA). As noted by scholar David Suárez (2007), this sphere allows its thousands of members—"through discourse and active reflection"—to "practice, negotiate, refine, and mold HRE" (66). Populated by many government officials and staff of UN agencies as well as educators and human rights activists globally, this online community has encouraged discursive engagement on various issues of HRE and has played a significant role in facilitating international discussions on the topic. Since many posts are from practitioners seeking advice, materials, or input, the online community can influence HRE practice as well.

With the global diffusion of ideas related to teaching and learning for human rights, different scholars have proposed various models for human rights education. Felisa Tibbitts (2002, 2017) posits a three-tiered model for human rights education that explores differing levels of implementation by distinct actors. Tibbitts differentiates between *the socialization approach of values and awareness of human rights* that can be utilized in formal and nonformal settings to introduce learners into basic knowledge about human rights; *the accountability or professional development approach* for those working directly with victims of rights abuses (e.g. police, health workers); and the more *activist transformation approach*, which offers a holistic understanding of human rights knowledge, attitudes, and actions (Tibbitts 2017). This model suggests productive areas for researchers and practitioners to examine the frameworks for analyzing such action.

Bajaj (2011) has argued elsewhere for the importance of documenting the varying ideologies of human rights education initiatives as they have proliferated across the globe in order to understand the relevance of the particular model adopted. Depending on relationships to power and conditions of marginalization, the perceived and actual outcomes of human rights education may differ based on social location (Bajaj 2012). Some programs, particularly those adopted at national and international levels or in sites of relative privilege, may discuss global citizenship as an outcome. In conflict settings, coexistence and respect for difference may be prioritized. In disenfranchised communities, HRE may be a strategy for transformative action and individual as well as collective empowerment (Bajaj 2011; Tibbitts 2002, 2017).

Critics have noted that the overly "declarationist" approach of HRE—that anchors itself in normative conceptions of rights—limits the field's emancipatory potential since it fails to consider broader debates in the field of human rights (Keet 2007). Scholars and practitioners have also increasingly advocated for critical (Keet 2007), transformative (Bajaj 2011, 2012; Cislaghi, Gillespie, & Macki 2017; Tibbitts 2005), and decolonial (Zemyblas 2020) forms of human rights education that take into consideration the distinct social locations and forms of marginalization faced by different groups in order for educational strategies to be more holistic, relevant, and effective.

Initiatives working toward human rights education tend to fuse Freirean notions of consciousness raising with the philosophical tradition of cosmopolitanism, as scholars have noted (Bajaj 2014; Bajaj, Cislaghi, & Mackie 2016; Meintjes 1997; Osler & Starkey 2010; Tibbitts 2002). Paulo Freire's (1970) notion of *conscientization* results from individuals—often those from disadvantaged groups—analyzing conditions of inequality collectively with others, and then, acting and reflecting on this analysis to inspire new action to overcome situations of oppression and subordination. Cosmopolitanism is a philosophical position that posits a shared human community and a global notion of citizenship and belonging (Appiah 2007b). Pairing these philosophical orientations together results in local action and critical analysis in a cyclical fashion (a la Freire) informed by global solidarity and connection (as is posited in some versions of cosmopolitanism). Some scholars have termed this type of HRE "transformative human rights education" (THRED) and have documented its principles and components across formal and nonformal settings (Bajaj, Cislaghi, & Mackie 2016; Bajaj 2017a; Hantzopoulos, 2016).

For such transformative HRE approaches, the following is a basic theory of change developed that might unite the purpose of human rights education for empowerment efforts (in its ideal form though, in practice, it may look different). It draws on Freire's notions of critical consciousness and ideas of global citizenship (Bajaj 2017b) and is visualized in Figure 3.1:

(a) Learners (in formal or nonformal settings) learn about a larger imagined moral community where human rights understandings offer a shared language;

(b) Learners question a social or cultural practice that does not fit within the global framework;

(c) Learners identify allies (teachers, peers, community activists, NGOs) to amplify one's voice along with other strategies for influencing positive social change (Bajaj 2017b).

While this theory of change can account for the way in which transformative human rights education is conceptualized, there are often many tensions and contradictions in actual practice—akin to arguments put forth by scholars of critical and decolonial peace education. These frictions include grappling with strategies to deal with the unintended consequences of human rights education and related corresponding action and unpacking the ways in which rights language is co-opted for entirely different ends (Bajaj 2012; Khoja-Moolji 2014; Mejias, 2017; Wahl 2014). Additionally, nation-states and policymakers have diverse reasons to take on human rights education—that may or may not include a transformative vision. These are areas that the field of human rights education must continue to engage with.

In the field of HRE, scholars use various methodological approaches to look at different levels of implementation and operation. Similarly, with practice, there are simultaneous efforts, likely going on somewhere in the world at this moment, to advocate for government adoption of HRE and to disseminate local understandings of rights as a means to resist dominant and oppressive forces. In the academic realm, there are several milestones worth mentioning that have advanced the institutionalization of the field: the establishment of academic programs in human rights and HRE (such as the first Masters of Arts in Human Rights Education at the University of

Figure 3.1 Participatory Dimensions of Transformative Human Rights Education. *Source: Reprinted from* Advancing Transformative Human Rights Education (Bajaj, Cislaghi, and Mackie 2016).

San Francisco in 2013) and the creation of academic journals and other publishing venues for scholarship on HRE (such as the *International Journal of Human Rights Education* and the *Human Rights Education Review* over the past decade, as well as the first-of-its-kind book series on peace and human rights education with Bloomsbury that this book launches). There have also been increasing academic research and partnerships with numerous grassroots efforts to educate marginalized communities about their rights across the globe. Approaches can be explicit (e.g., a human rights class) or implicit (e.g., integrated across other subjects) and can be within designated learning spaces, like schools, or training programs or in nonformal spaces, like museums or community centers. At each level—whether in scholarship, advocacy, or grassroots practice—different ideologies and theoretical frameworks guide the approach to human rights education.

Conceptual Orientations

There are diverse theoretical and conceptual orientations that underpin the field of HRE. As with the different HRE models discussed earlier, these theories examine human rights education from distinct vantage points. It is important to tease out what lies beneath a decision to incorporate human rights education because such analysis—as with Galtung's (1969) conceptualizations of different forms of violence that is central in peace education—offers insights into what rights are privileged, what such efforts signal, and how HRE is utilized in a given context. In the scholarly literature, a divergence of ideologies is not as pronounced as is a proliferation of approaches, and different scholars find diverse aspects of the field worthwhile of attention.

As shown in Table 3.2, human rights education theories can be categorized in three sets, which may or may not overlap depending on the focus of a given study. Scholars of neo-institutional theory argue that human rights education is a result of educational convergence (Ramirez, Suarez, & Meyer 2007; Meyer, Bromley-Martin, & Ramirez 2010; Suárez 2007): a process that reduces local distinctions within education systems. This means that policy discourse and textbooks converge toward normative human rights frameworks. In their research, scholars undertake cross-national analyses of the institutionalization of the field by examining phenomena like the proliferation of publications on HRE, the emergence of similar HRE policies and organizations across contexts, and the representation of human rights in textbooks (Russell, Sirota, & Ahmed 2019). Russell and Suárez (2017) note that "the human rights education movement has evolved from a global discourse linked to the international human rights framework to a broader education movement incorporating concrete policy changes and actions in national and local contexts across diverse nations" (30–31).

Scholars committed to the second set of theories in Table 3.2 foreground cultural or historical context in their analysis of human rights education. Another common feature of studies conducted by Marxist, postcolonial, and critical theorists is their investigation of power imbalances, particularly in their questioning of the universality of human rights and their emphasis on the importance of cultural and historical context when teaching human rights (Al-Daraweesh & Snauwaert 2015; Burke 2013; Baxi 1997). Critiques about the Western nature of human rights and notions of individual rights within the rise of neoliberalism also emerge from this theoretical category.

Scholars who utilize theories in the first part of the third set of perspectives, as shown in Table 3.2, base their studies on the concept of Freirean critical consciousness (Freire 1970), which builds on a collaborative and dialogical cycle of praxis—reflection, analysis, and humanizing action—to advance collective liberation from social and political oppression. Therefore, these scholars conceptualize human rights education as an emancipatory and transformative process that is focused on dismantling local power asymmetries through grassroots activism. Studies that emerge from this set of theories are classroom- and community-based and focus on the immediate and specific issues grassroots communities are facing.

Another set of scholarship that emerges, focused on classroom, community, professional, and institutional settings, comprises those that take a more skeptical look at the influence and use of human rights education, as seen in the second part of Group 3 in the table. For example, Wahl (2016) examines how police officers in India utilize a certificate course in human rights "to refute its core principles, arguing that their interpretation of human rights should replace more standard interpretations" (293–4). Similarly, Mejias (2017) examines how stakeholders at a London school that has adopted Amnesty International's Human Rights Friendly Schools framework co-opt the language and understandings of human rights to advance a diverse set of agendas.

As a way of visual categorization, Table 3.2 represents an overview of the different theoretical strands of human rights education. While all of the HRE categories in Table 3.2 explain different aspects of the phenomenon of HRE, theories and scholarship in the first strand focus on policies, documents, and texts relevant to HRE; theories from the second strand are more context-oriented, bringing into focus the Western character of rights discourses; and theories from the third strand are classroom-, community-, and organization-based, examining pedagogy and possibilities for transformation as well as some of the pitfalls and tensions of these approaches. Scholarship in each of these theoretical groupings has advanced the field and examined the different dimensions of human rights education from its rise, to its adoption, to its sometimes-transformative and sometimes-contested implementation in diverse global settings.

Global Scholarship About HRE in Practice

Scholarship in the field of human rights education has been conceptual, empirical, and multidisciplinary. Contemporary scholarship that examines

Table 3.2 Theoretical Underpinnings of Human Rights Education Scholarship

	Focus of HRE	Key Concepts	Theoretical Underpinnings	Fundamental Argument	Scholars & Selected Representative Works
Group 1	Law; Policy; Textbooks; Educational Systems	Policy; declarations; discourse; convergence	Neo-institutional theory; convergence theory	*Human rights seen as global legal and moral consensus; education systems and textbooks converge toward these frameworks.*	Bromley (2014) Meyer, Bromley, & Ramirez (2010) Nakagawa & Wotipka (2016) Ramirez, Meyer, & Suarez (2007) Russell & Suárez (2017) Suarez (2007) Tarrow (1992)
Group 2	Discourse Ideology; Knowledge Production	Historical analyses; asymmetries of power; decolonization of human rights and HRE	Marxist theory; critical theory; postcolonial, poststructural, & decolonial approaches	*Culture, context, and historical relations of power need to mediate any and all forms of HRE and schooling.*	Al-Daraweesh & Snauwaert (2015) Baxi (1997) Cardenas (2005) Keet (2007) Zembylas (2017, 2020)
Group 3a	Classrooms; Communities; Schools; Professions & Other Settings where HRE is implemented	Transformation; empowerment; praxis-oriented; dialogue; solidarity; agency; collective action & strategic resistance	Critical theory; Freirean critical consciousness; postcolonial and decolonial approaches; "Indigenous rights education" (Sumida-Huaman 2017)	*HRE should be driven by local actors, rooted in community, and contextually adapted in order to foster individual and collective transformation.*	Bajaj (2012, 2018) Cislaghi, Gillespie, & Mackie (2017) Hantzopoulos (2016) Holland & Martin (2017) Katz & Spero (2015) Magendzo (2005) Osler & Starkey (2010) Sumida Huaman (2017) Spreen & Monaghan (2017) Tibbitts (2001)

| Group 3b | Co-optation; micropolitics; contestation of meanings; "neoliberal entanglements" of HRE (Khoja-Moolji 2014); reflective inquiry; oppositional resistance | "Ideology critique" (Coysh 2017); "colonialism of rights" (Douzinas 2007); "critical postmodern pedagogy" (Keet 2010) | *Human rights education can be co-opted and manipulated for diverse agendas at the local level, leveraging its global popularity for legitimacy.* | Bajaj (2016b) Coysh (2017) Keet (2010, 2017) Khoja-Moolji (2014) Mejias (2017) Wahl (2014) |

Adapted and Reprinted from Bajaj and Mabona (2021).

human rights education in practice is summarized in this section to offer readers a sense of the breadth and key learnings from core texts in the field. We exclude scholarship that is more prescriptive in terms of advice for educators because it often sets out an ideal but does not necessarily engage with what happens in contexts where human rights education is underway. Given our own positioning as scholars in the field in the third area as illustrated in Table 3.2—and our advocacy for further empirical research in the field that examines the complex realities within classrooms, organizations, and communities where human rights education is being localized—we offer a review of key scholarship primarily in this theoretical area.

Popular and Nonformal Education for Human Rights

Popular education—a participatory and dialogical process where colearners start from their own experience to generate new knowledge and understanding of issues—is a complementary pedagogy for human rights education. Popular education draws on Paulo Freire's (1970) ideas about creating a horizontal dynamic between educators and learners where dialogue based in lived experiences shapes the learning process. Popular education can be utilized in community-based settings, particularly where there are low-literacy levels, using images or participatory activities. Augusto Boal (1993) and colleagues developed the *Theater of the Oppressed*, a methodology of participatory theater that can be used to generate meaningful discussion and deliberation on social problems and inequalities. Many human rights educators—and peace educators—have drawn on popular education techniques and principles to foster discussion about rights and justice in diverse settings, and scholars have also studied such efforts in distinct contexts. Popular education principles of dialogue and dialogical learning have also infused efforts in formal education, especially in settings where the hierarchies and silences of authoritarian, colonial, or otherwise-oppressive rule necessitate the development of participatory strategies for authentic learning.

Groundbreaking scholarship in the field of human rights education in the 1990s emerged from Latin America immediately following the transition from authoritarian dictatorships to democracy, for example in Chile. Abraham Magendzo, a pioneering human rights education scholar, discussed how even before the transition to democracy from Augusto Pinochet's repressive rule (1973–90)—"at a time when simply talking about human rights in Chile was a crime that could be severely punished" (Magendzo 1994: 251)—he was active with others committed to popular education for discussing human rights education. He notes, "Many of the educators participating in seminars were people who had been tortured, kept in jail for long periods, humiliated and denigrated in horrible manners. I came to the conclusion that when democracy was recovered, human rights education should be the main objective of education" (Magendzo 2005: 138). Along with groups of educators, he developed teacher trainings, sat on committees of the Ministry of Education during the transition to democracy, and was part of processes related to the Chilean Commission on Truth and Reconciliation in 1991.

In discussing this work, Magendzo (1994) notes some of the impediments of the school system that human rights education could help address, but that also could serve as a hurdle, in transitioning popular education for human rights into the formal schooling context.

> The aspects of school culture, teaching practice, the nature of teacher-student interactions, and the deeply rooted authoritarianism in schools, are to be questioned. We want to disclose the school's underlying messages, the mechanism used for the reproduction of social inequalities, and the unfair distribution of knowledge . . . we say: let us make room for human rights in the open curriculum, and from there we shall gain access to the hidden one. (253)

The introduction of human rights into the educational system, particularly since most societies have utilized schooling for indoctrination and as a tool for reproducing the status and norms of the dominant classes (Freire 1970), can also open spaces for the sharing of human rights experiences—whether students' families have been victims, perpetrators, or bystanders.

Educators as well have often lived through traumatic conflict, and trainings can be spaces of collective sharing and the deepening of collective memory toward healing. Magendzo notes that teachers can "use this opportunity to speak about things that have been repressed for many years . . . [and that] all kinds of lived experiences come up in a torrent of words and there is an uncontrollable desire to be listened to" (1994: 257–8). Through teacher agency, critical pedagogy, and creating space for the creation of collective memory—even if contested—within human rights education, HRE scholars and practitioners in Latin America (in Chile and elsewhere) have advanced the field's understandings of the pedagogies and processes of participatory and democratic human rights education.

Community organizations have also utilized popular education in settings characterized by authoritarianism, violent conflict, and deep social inequalities. Documenting organizations that work at the nexus of peacebuilding and human rights education in five national contexts (Mexico, Colombia, Liberia, Senegal, and Sierra Leone), Holland and Martin (2017) examine organizations serving marginalized communities, such as displaced women in Colombia and rural communities in postconflict Liberia. They examine how participatory human rights education, for example with street children unable to attend school in Mexico, can serve as a source of critical reflection on unequal social conditions through the Project Melel program, which they studied. Through weekly learning circles, children reflect on their lives, rooted in discussions of the UN Convention on the Rights of the Child (UNCRC).

> Specific rights topics contained in the CRC that are identified by the children as being especially relevant to their daily lives include rights against physical abuse and their right to attend school apart from their needing to work. The children learn broader human rights concepts, such as gender equality and governmental responsibility to ensure the protection of citizens' rights. Because the majority of the children in Project Melel are of Totzil ethnic background, the project contextualizes children's rights by relating them back to the [Indigenous] Totzil concept of *lekil kuxlejal*, a good life. (Holland and Martin 2017: 275)

Project Melel focuses on children who are extremely vulnerable to violence and are unable to access formal schooling. Many nonformal approaches reach highly marginalized populations whose access to formal schooling has been or is severely limited.

Through participatory research in West Africa, Cislaghi, Mackie, and Gillespie (2017) have documented the popular education approaches of the NGO Tostan, whose mission is to "empower communities to develop and achieve their vision for the future and inspires large-scale movements leading to dignity for all" (Tostan n.d.). In their research, the authors found that through Tostan's Community Empowerment Program (CEP), which lasts thirty months in numerous villages throughout West Africa, "rural communities came to advance human rights in their larger communities and beyond; they did so in a way that aligned local practices with specific human rights in efforts to actualize their vision of community well-being" (253).

The modules of Tostan's curriculum include themes of democracy, human rights, conflict transformation, and health and are offered in the first language of villagers by a local facilitator who lives with the community for the duration of the multiyear program. Two classes of twenty to fifty participants (one class for adults and the other for adolescents) take place three times a week for two hours, and "both curriculum and pedagogy draw on participants' cultural background, their daily experiences, and their existing knowledge and abilities. To increase the reach of the program, facilitators require each participant to share the new knowledge acquired in [the course] with one 'adopted learner,' a nonparticipating member of their family or group of friends" (254). The pedagogy includes participatory discussions often emerging from the discussion of a "generative theme" (Freire 1970)—usually an image or an illustrated local proverb—put up on a poster in the middle of the circle; discussions, role-plays (drawing on Augusto Boal's [1993] Theater of the Oppressed techniques where participants can intervene in ongoing skits), and dialogues ensue to unpack the theme of the day's session. Tostan's curricular innovations and decades of efforts in nonformal human rights education have resulted in many communities increasing girls' participation in education, the abandonment of female genital cutting in villages where it was previously practiced, and greater health outcomes as well (Tostan n.d.).

Transformative Human Rights Education in K–12 Settings

Many approaches to human rights education focus on curricular content and textbook reforms, which demonstrate the rise of human rights education discourses and reforms in global educational policymaking. There are important scholarly contributions that document the rise of human rights education through textbook reforms across the globe (Meyer, Bromley-Martin, & Ramirez 2010; Russell and Suarez 2017; Russell, Sirota, & Ahmed 2019). But such scholarship also notes the limits of textbooks in a more comprehensive human rights education; for example, scholars have found that "although human rights discourse is prevalent in South African textbooks, in general it is limited to conveying knowledge about human rights rather than instigating students to act on behalf of protecting their rights" (Russell, Sirota, & Ahmed 2019: 19).

Human rights education that integrates cognitive as well affective and activist-oriented components has been termed "transformative human rights education" (THRED) (Bajaj, Cislaghi, & Mackie 2016), differentiating it from the more superficial and normative forms of HRE that characterize some efforts in research, policy, and practice. Scholars have also noted that the pathway to achieve such forms of critical and transformative HRE must be "decolonizing" or "decolonial" (Coysh 2017; Williams & Bermeo 2020; Zembylas 2017, 2020), as will be discussed later in this chapter. Such approaches focus on more critical analyses of social relations to infuse studies of the gap between rights and actual realities that communities face (Bajaj, Canlas, & Argenal 2017). In formal school settings, transformative human rights education has been discussed primarily in middle and secondary schools, training institutes, and colleges and universities. Through sustained empirical research that focuses on the content, methods, pedagogies, and the impact on both students and educators, scholars have contributed to our understandings of the possibility for human rights learning within formal educational settings.

The role of the educator and facilitator in transformative human rights education efforts is not only to impart information but also to build the capacity for learners to believe that they are worthy of rights when their communities may have been marginalized for generations as well as to nurture the social action that may result from learning about deep-seated inequalities. Human rights education, oriented as such and rooted in Freirean conceptions of critical consciousness raising for social change, has the potential to foster teaching and learning for individual and social transformation.

In research in India, Bajaj (2012) examines a three-year school-based program offering human rights education to students in grades six, seven, and eight through a robust partnership between thousands of schools and an Indian NGO, the Institute for Human Rights Education (IHRE). Through an in-depth case study of the program across several states in India, interviewing hundreds of teachers, students, and staff members, Bajaj highlights the ways the program addresses caste and gender violence, child labor, communalism, among other pressing social issues in the local and national contexts, and their impact on both students and educators (IHRE's pedagogical approaches are discussed in Chapter 4 of this book). The organization, through a community-based strategy that stems from its human rights legal and advocacy work, centers the voices and experiences of marginalized peoples in India, primarily Dalit (formerly called "untouchable") and Adivasi (Indigenous) communities. The "transformative" dimensions of the work emerge from this community-based strategy that prioritizes lived experiences, local examples of activism, and deep connections to social movements. Through this example of "explicit" human rights education—

where rights are taught by trained teachers through a weekly course over three years—students from marginalized groups begin to reconsider notions of equality and democratic citizenship, as do those from slightly more privileged groups who understand how to exert "coalitional agency" to work in solidarity to speak out against injustices (Bajaj 2012).

In the United States, two examples of transformative human rights education in formal settings are discussed by Hantzopoulos (2016) and Spreen and Monaghan (2017). Hantzopoulos's research on the Humanities Preparatory Academy ("Prep"), a public high school in NYC, offers both "implicit" and "explicit" human rights education, at the intersection of critical peace education, through the functions of a unique school rooted in dignity, agency, and justice (as has been discussed some in Chapter 2 of this book). Through restorative practices, town hall meetings, and dialogical learning, the principles of human rights education are brought to life in the school (Hantzopoulos 2016). The school promotes elective courses and study trips that focus on human rights explicitly, and students are exposed to concepts and issues to analyze the gaps between rights and realities on the ground in their own and other communities. Students responded favorably to the approach, structure, and environment of the school: "between teachers, students, everyone interacted with each other, everyone looked at one another as equals and it created a true sense of democracy within a school which is quite rare" (Hantzopoulos 2012c: 39). Such curricular and pedagogical orientations that aligned with transformative human rights education influenced students' worldviews and attitudes toward social change as well; for example, one student noted the following:

> One of the most important lessons that I learned was that activism did not have to be only big issues that you hear about on TV or marching with signs, but could be as small as helping someone in the neighborhood, or making the school look nicer. By making activism possible, Prep instilled in me the need to always be working towards positive change. (Hantzopoulos 2016: 137)

While longitudinal research that examines the longer-term influences of transformative human rights education over time once out of the protection of such spaces is needed, the results from research such as Hantzopoulos's that studied student and alumni experiences certainly indicate the benefits of whole-school approaches to human rights education, including in the long term.

Spreen and Monaghan (2017) discuss a unique collaborative action-research project involving diverse high school students, university students, and professors (in law and education) in Virginia. Spreen and Monaghan explore the limitations of traditional, normative approaches to history and civic education and demonstrate the strengths and possibilities for critical, rights-based approaches in enabling high school-age learners to explore their communities. They profile a high school course called "Becoming a Global Citizen," in which recently arrived refugee and migrant students (from Africa, the Middle East, Europe, Asia, and Latin America) were partnered with a diverse group of US-born students (who were from various racial, ethnic, and socioeconomic backgrounds) to learn about human rights and civic engagement. Through the course, students got to know and humanized one another, understanding rights through the relationships they formed and through lessons and projects that engaged in community action. For example, the authors recount the story of how one student used the content of the global citizenship course to stand up to an infringement of her and her friends' rights (all of them were students of color) during an unwarranted stop by the police:

> Lexis recounts that she and her friends were becoming increasingly anxious as the officer badgered them for more and different forms of identification, she thought back to the stop-and-frisk activity we had in class the previous week and reflected "I knew he didn't have the right to do this" . . . Lexis told the officer that he could not detain her or her friends, then asked for his name and badge number, and let him know she was going to report him for harassment. She did exactly that and several weeks later, after the police had launched an investigation into the matter following the complaint, the officer was suspended from active duty and Lexis was issued a formal apology. Reflecting on the event later in the classroom, Lexis explained, "it was because of this class . . . because we had talked about it and what to do if something like this happened, that I knew how to take a stand and knew what my rights are." (Spreen & Monaghan 2017: 309)

As with the examples of other transformative human rights education and in the theory of change presented earlier in this chapter, young people identifying a violation of a rights issue in their community and taking action can offer them a meaningful lesson in human rights, particularly when it results in some sort of positive change.

Data from research on schools and programs that seek to fuse human rights with participatory pedagogies to foster transformative agency and critical consciousness offer scholars and practitioners insights about the possibilities of this form of human rights education. Examples in the research of scholars such as Bajaj, Hantzopoulos, Spreen, and Monaghan suggest that certain pockets exist whether in elective courses (Spreen & Monaghan 2017), mission-driven and social justice-oriented small high schools (Hantzopoulos 2012c, 2016), after-school programs (Bajaj, Canlas, & Argenal 2017), and NGO-run programs that have official authorization to operate in schools (Bajaj 2012). In such settings, alignment of ideologies, classroom practices, and student outcomes facilitates a transformative impact; but, at times, school structures and institutional mandates often impede this form of HRE. The following section discusses some of the tensions that emerge when the meanings of HRE are contested or co-opted.

Contested Meanings of Human Rights Education

Teaching about human rights raises expectations and demands on the state, whether such learning occurs in formal (educational institutions), informal (in families and communities), or nonformal contexts (in organizations, museums, or other programs). As political scientist Cardenas (2005) notes, "Human rights education (or the construction of a human rights culture) is inherently revolutionary: if implemented effectively, it has the potential to generate social opposition, alongside rising demands for justice and accountability" (364). Understanding the power of human rights education if implemented effectively, there are many reasons why participants/learners in programs resist what is being taught or why implementers of such programs subvert the "revolutionary" potential of HRE to co-opt such programs and policies for other purposes. A rich body of scholarship has examined these disjunctures, tensions, and contestations in human rights education (Khoja-Moolji 2014; Mejias 2017; Wahl 2017).

Mejias (2017) draws on his extensive ethnographic research in a London secondary school to discuss gaps between the vision, implementation, and outcomes of Amnesty International's whole-school human rights education initiative, Human Rights Friendly Schools (HRFS)—a program that operates in dozens of schools globally to infuse human rights principles into every aspect of school life through implicit and explicit approaches. Mejias discusses how, rather than aligning school practices with HRE, the school used the program and affiliation with it as a political tool to showcase during national inspections. Later, disgruntled teachers and students utilized HRE to destabilize the school's leadership team and, ultimately, the school itself. The promise of HRE was held out in the face of a wide gap between rights and actual realities in a contested school setting. Through an examination of the "micropolitical" activity in the school (such as through rumors, gossip, and strategic alliances), Mejias explores some of the limits of human rights education discourse when co-opted by various actors for divergent purposes. In Mejias's case study, the HRE initiative embraced by the school was ultimately abandoned after the micropolitical activity resulted in the ouster of the head teacher who initially supported the program.

In research on a tertiary certificate program on human rights for adult learners completed via distance education in northern India, Wahl (2017) explores the perspectives of police officers who participate as a means to advance their career prospects. Wahl's research discusses the "moral universe inhabited by law enforcers who support or use torture, and the implications for how they respond to activism and education to protect human rights" (Wahl 2017: 19). In analyzing law enforcers' responses to the content of their human rights course, Wahl "reveals the micro-dynamics of resistance among the ground-level agents who are charged with upholding global norms" and further "shows the plasticity of moral vocabularies" (20). Through their own negotiation with conceptions of rights, the officers interviewed demonstrate how they reframe human rights to fit existing or preferred worldviews.

In neighboring Pakistan, Khoja-Moolji (2014) discusses how over time, the language of human rights has become part of the accepted "common sense" vis-à-vis neoliberal conceptions of citizenship. She examines the experiences of young women in a summer program titled "Women Leaders of Tomorrow" (WLT), which espoused individual notions of leadership as a proxy for promoting social change in communities that the participants hailed from. Khoja-Moolji reflects on participant responses to the program— which the author and a colleague designed—to examine their "resistances, co-option, and self-stylisations" of the participants at WLT" (115). Khoja-Moolji further notes that participants

> resisted aspects of it that attempted to de-link them from their communities or destabilised structures that were critical sources of security for them. These instances of resistance and the unfolding of the globalist human rights discourse in a local setting direct me to call for a re-conceptualisation of HRE in postcolonial contexts that is multiple, contingent, and fluid. We, thus, observe mutations of HRE as opposed to uni-directional transfers of knowledge. (104)

In this case, even when programs are designed by members of a community, the circulating discourses about HRE influence program design and funding opportunities. The author further argues that "HRE can be re-conceptualised to include an interrogation of its assumptions about citizenship, the history that gives it its normative force, and the power relations that it may (re) produce" (116). The centrality of power and power relations defines this strand of HRE scholarship that examines the contestation of meanings, functions, and discourses of human rights in a particular context; understandings of power also infuse calls for a more decolonial approach to HRE, as the following section discusses.

Decolonial Directions

Scholarship on human rights education has interrogated Western conceptions of human rights, as well as questioned notions of the "human" in such discourses. In his afterword to a book on human rights pedagogies in the United States (Katz & Spero 2015), Yang (2015) suggests that "for HRE to be decolonizing depends on our willingness to denaturalize the category of Human," drawing on the work of Sylvia Wynter (1994) and referring to the status of propertied men as the default template of citizens in settler-colonies such as the United States. Keet (2018) echoes this call to decolonize HRE by questioning it "through incessant critique" (27) and reformulations that "engage with the erosion of citizenship, democracy, and human rights under the annihilating influence of neoliberalism's stealth revolution" (28).

Further building on the call for decolonizing human rights education, Michalinos Zembylas argues for the need to interrogate the premises of human rights:

> In order for HRE to become more "critical" (Keet 2017) and "transformative" (Bajaj, Cislaghi, and Mackie 2016), it needs to go beyond the epistemological and ontological grounding inherent in the dominant human rights regime. For this to happen, we need to develop HRE theory and practice that go beyond critical pedagogies that highlight the human as the unit of liberation (Yang 2015) . . . Decolonization of the HRE curriculum, therefore, means to offer accounts of human rights that would force European thinking and knowledge to confront its barbarism and coloniality. To achieve this, the decolonizing approach needs to embrace three critical curriculum approaches: anti-essentialism, contrapuntal readings, and ethical solidarity. (Zembylas 2017: 36, 37 and 46)

Zembylas further questions the "trappings of sentimentality" that substitute pity for solidarity in examining the experiences of those suffering human rights abuses (46). Zembylas links such "trappings" of sentimentality as an off-shoot of colonial logics that center inaction and passivity as opposed to solidarity and agency in struggles for social justice. He also cautions against the strategic deployment of emotion to support one-sided historical narratives through human rights education, citing his own work in Cyprus with teachers involved in education toward reconciliation between the two sides of the divided island.

Further interrogating colonial narratives, Coysh (2017), in work on grassroots HRE initiatives in Tanzania, discusses how the perspectives of experts from urban centers and from overseas are privileged when defining what rights and approaches of HRE will be discussed and implemented. Overriding Indigenous knowledges, these experts deploy forms of HRE that follow the "declarationist" approach that adheres to Eurocentric/Western conceptions of rights (Keet 2007). In looking ahead to the potential decolonial directions of the field of HRE, Coysh asserts that "HRE discourse should invoke the multiple discourses of resistance and action that are connected to pre-existing forms of Indigenous knowledge and cultural resources of communities. This requires rethinking HRE discourse to one that is more concerned with unearthing the subjugated knowledges, and founded upon the characteristics of questioning and critique" (Coysh 2017: 158–9).

In considering how Indigenous knowledges and ways of being can inform HRE, Sumida-Huaman (2017) posits the framework for an "Indigenous Rights Education" (IRE), which prioritizes discourses of place rights, language rights, and the protection of lands as well as physical and intellectual heritage. The author calls for a complex examination of the histories of schooling as a process of colonization and domination, and the need to examine possibilities for IRE that exist oftentimes in out-of-school and intergenerational spaces where cultural knowledge is transmitted. In-school spaces can also be transformed toward Indigenous rights education based on community priorities rooted in Indigenous knowledge systems, particularly related to "human and environmental sustainability" (25). Central to this model of HRE for Indigenous communities is self-determination.

Further discussing a critical and decolonial vision for HRE, Steinborn and Nusbaum (2019) call for a "cripping"—an inclusive term referring to the ways members of the disabled community and allies have responded to forms of oppression and exclusion—of human rights education to "visibilize" disability in human rights praxis. The authors contend that "if HRE scholars took seriously the work of disability studies in education, human rights overall could become more accessible and utilitarian for all people whose multiple identities and complex, politicized body/minds are not accounted for in the UN's seminal documents" (2019: 6). Steinborn and Nusbaum further develop a reading list with the goal of focusing on "activists' micro-contexts" to foster knowledge and discussion about disability rights that have long been rendered invisible in human rights and HRE discourses (9).

Decolonizing, critical, and transformative HRE necessarily requires a centering of marginalized voices and a decentering of the Eurocentric and neoliberal conceptions of individual rights that infuse the human rights framework. With overlap between the critical, transformative, and decolonial approaches to HRE, there are calls for an interrogation of the colonial logics that frame schooling as an institution as well as human rights as a field. The decolonial project for human rights education offers scholars and students a productive framework in which to project and direct future research that can push the field forward toward increasingly critically engaged and transformative directions.

Conclusion

This chapter has offered an overview of the foundations, theories, models, frameworks, and global scholarship on human rights education. Scholars have discussed how human rights education gets localized and how international educational policies and textbooks have increasingly featured content on human rights. The following chapter offers a case study that discusses how transformative human rights education, through a popular education program for adult women in Bangladesh and a school-based HRE program for marginalized youth in India, has been contextualized in diverse ways in the South Asian region. Readers can engage with specific models of HRE through the case study to understand better what human rights education looks like in practice, undergirded by the field's principles, commitments, and trajectories.

4

Human Rights Education in Practice

Examples from South Asia[1]

Chapter Outline

South Asian Education	82
From Sticks to Students' Rights: School-Based HRE in India	84
"Barefoot lawyers" as Human Rights Educators in Bangladesh	89
Discussion and Concluding Thoughts	92

In this chapter, we delve into how human rights education (HRE) has been localized in South Asia and made into the *vernacular* (Merry 2006) to build on the concepts, models, and histories discussed in Chapter 3. The South Asian region, comprised of the diverse nations of Afghanistan, Bangladesh, Bhutan, India, the Maldives, Nepal, Pakistan and Sri Lanka, is home to one-fifth of the world's population. Educational realities differ widely across the region: for example, 65 percent of girls in Bangladesh are married before the age of eighteen (HRW 2015), while, at the same time, each year approximately 200,000 of students from affluent Indian families pursue higher education in North America, Europe, and Australia (Clark 2013). Widening social inequalities within and across nations further distinguish the educational experiences of youth throughout the region (World Bank 2015), including their ability to enjoy the rights enshrined in international documents (Bajaj 2017a).

There is a long history of commitment to human rights in the South Asian region, although gaps exist between human rights policies and actual practices on the ground. Anticolonial movements espoused (at-that-time radical) goals of equality, nondiscrimination, and dignity—pillars of international human rights (Bajaj 2017a). The adoption in 1948 of the UN Universal Declaration of Human Rights (UDHR), arguably the cornerstone document of the global rights framework, occurred around the same time as the independence of many South Asian nations from British rule. Indeed, three of South Asia's eight nations were among the original forty-eight votes in favor of the UDHR (Afghanistan, India, and Pakistan), among the few independent nations at that time in the Global South.

From 1948 to the present day, there has been a rise in attention to education as a core component of human development, dignity, and basic rights. Article 26 of the Universal Declaration of Human Rights guarantees a right to education, and one that "strengthens respect for human rights and fundamental freedoms." Children's right to an education was further codified through the Education for All conferences (1990 & 2000), the Millennium & Sustainable Development Goals (2000 & 2015), and other global commitments. Among other evidence of global support for education, in 2014, two advocates for the right to education—both from South Asia— were awarded the Nobel Peace Prize: Malala Yousafzai, a Pakistani adolescent brutally shot for advocating for girls' right to go to school, and Indian activist Kailash Satyarthi, who has campaigned for an end to child labor for decades and is the cofounder of the Global Campaign for Education.

This direction is striking and noteworthy since less than a century ago, education was seen in many places as a privilege rather than a right. For instance, at India and Pakistan's independence in 1947, a mere 16 percent of the populace was literate (Rana & Sugden 2013). The 2014 Nobel Peace Prize signaled the ongoing evolution within global consciousness that the right to education is an aspect of comprehensive and sustainable peace, and its denial is a grave social injustice (Bajaj 2017a). This chapter focuses on a less-discussed component of the international human rights framework: the right to an education that fosters and promotes human rights and that prepares active participants for democratic life: in other words, "human rights education."

This chapter explores how human rights education as a global educational movement is taken up locally by educators, activists and non-governmental organizations (NGOs) in South Asia. As has been discussed in the previous chapter, human rights education assumes various forms, depending on context, ideologies, and location (Bajaj 2012; Tibbitts 2002, 2017; Tsolakis

2013). Transformative human rights education—rooted in critical analyses of power and social inequalities—has been developed by nonstate actors more than by government school systems, specifically by NGOs, social movements, and community-based educators (Bajaj, Cislaghi, & Mackie 2016). As a result, this chapter zooms in on two examples of transformative human rights education in the South Asian context that seek—in different locally contextualized ways—to interrogate power asymmetries and offer members of marginalized groups the opportunity to envision and demand equal rights (Bajaj 2017a). The first example is a school-based program designed by a human rights organization (People's Watch through its Institute for Human Rights Education) that trains teachers to offer a weekly human rights course in grades six through eight across India. The second example is a human rights education and legal empowerment program for poor, rural women in Bangladesh offered by the world's largest nongovernmental organization, BRAC (formerly an acronym for the Bangladesh Rural Advancement Committee; now, Building Resources Across Communities). The two cases presented here differ in approach, population, and context, but—as will be seen—both programs rely on well-trained teachers/facilitators who use innovative curriculum, effective participatory pedagogies, and strong relationships with learners to assist them in recognizing and confronting the injustices that surround their lives.

Human rights education has been discussed by some international and comparative education scholars as a product of growing educational convergence (Ramirez, Suarez, & Meyer 2007, Meyer, Bromley-Martin, & Ramirez 2010; Suarez 2007): a process through which systems look "strikingly similar" when looking downward from North to South (as cited in Krücken & Drori, 2010: 125). This, indeed, proves true at the level of global discourse, national policies, and textbook revisions (Meyer, Bromley-Martin, & Ramirez 2010). Research on HRE in South Asia and elsewhere, however, has shown that examining grassroots human rights education closely offers a more dynamic glimpse into how such global discourses and policies are strategically utilized and galvanized in securing support and legitimacy for radical educational projects that seek to empower marginalized communities (Bajaj 2012, 2017). And, in fact, when looking at educational programs in the Global South on their own terms—not through the gaze of the North—we can see dynamism and innovation that responds to local needs and realities, as well as contextually meaningful engagement with human rights frameworks.

South Asian Education

In South Asian educational systems, set up under British colonial rule, rote learning and what educational philosopher Paulo Freire (1970) referred to as "banking education" dominate; in this approach, children are seen as (passive) empty vessels to be filled with content by authoritarian teachers. Formal education was set up in colonial India (which then included the majority of the countries that now make up the South Asian subcontinent) to produce small cadres of "Anglicized Indians . . . [meaning] a class of persons Indian in blood and colour, but English in tastes, in opinions, in morals and in intellect" (Lord Macaulay, as cited in Evans 2002: 271), as intermediaries between the colonialists and the "masses" (Bajaj 2017a). Thus, Western education in South Asia was designed to reach a small proportion of the population: mostly young men of the then-small middle class. Unsurprisingly, in 1900, less than 6 percent of the population of colonial India and less than 1 percent of women and girls were literate (Chaudhary 2007). Despite independence from the British and the creation of various new nation-states in the mid-1900s, certain legacies lingered: the higher status afforded to English education, the predominance of rote learning, and a distinction between elite and mass education (Bajaj 2017a).

Despite these patterns, formal and nonformal education has also been conceived of as a site for resistance to unequal social conditions in South Asia. For example, independence leader Mohandas Gandhi's vision for education was to reorient education toward village life and the realities of the rural majority in order "to spearhead a silent revolution" (as cited in Bajaj 2010: 47). Newly independent India's first law minister, anticolonial and Dalit lawyer B.R. Ambedkar, who helped draft India's Constitution, viewed education as a force for social change; in the 1920s, Ambedkar founded an organization whose motto was to "Educate, Agitate, Organize" (Kadam 1991), a more radical iteration of the ideas of Ambedkar's former professor at Columbia University, John Dewey, and similar to the philosophies of Paulo Freire developed in subsequent decades, as discussed in Chapter 1.

Paulo Freire's theories of individual and collective empowerment through education for critical consciousness have traveled far and wide from South America (Freire was Brazilian and wrote *Pedagogy of the Oppressed* while in exile in Chile), to find resonance on the South Asian subcontinent (Bajaj 2017a). In South Asia, where Freire's work has been translated into multiple regional languages, progressive educators have been engaged with ideas of education for critical consciousness for many decades, preceding the recent rise of human rights education. For example, the adult literacy campaign in the Indian state of Kerala in the 1980s and 1990s, resulting in the state's near-universal literacy rates for men and women—far exceeding national levels—drew from Paulo Freire's ideas about literacy and popular education (Mayfield 2012), which had also been implemented successfully in postrevolutionary Cuba.

Although Freire was not considered a human rights educator per se, and his approaches are central to peace education as explained earlier, contemporary human rights education scholars and practitioners globally have drawn on his seminal writings to inform *how* the field approaches the teaching and learning of material related to human rights. By raising the "critical human rights consciousness" of learners (Meintjes 1997: 78) with analyses of social inequalities and historical forms of oppression, South Asian educators, such as those working for organizations profiled in this chapter like People's Watch and BRAC, seek to offer learners the ability to transform their own realities. It is important to note the specific influence Freire had on the founders of each of the organizations discussed in this chapter, though their specific approaches will be discussed in the following section. One of the founders of People's Watch (India), who oversaw the writing of the human rights education textbooks utilized in their program, taught (and helped translate into Tamil) Freire's works for decades. Further, posters with Freire's image and quotes written in local languages hang in the thousands of schools where the organization operates its human rights education program.

Many of Freire's books can also be found in BRAC's offices in Dhaka, Bangladesh, and the founders of the organization have noted the influence of his theories on their establishment of the organization. According to one of BRAC's early staff members: "In 1973, [BRAC's founder] [Fazle Hasan] Abed started reading Freire. His reading was quite revolutionary, and he also made me read *Wretched of the Earth* [by Franz Fanon] and *De-schooling Society* [by Ivan Illich]. And then we all got hooked on Freire, and we thought about how to use Freire's methods in our literacy work" (as cited in Smillie 2009: 154). Fazle Hasan Abed has further stated that poverty is a result of powerlessness and that BRAC's work is to enable poor people to "organise themselves so that they may change their lives" (BRAC 2014). Freire's ideas and theories undergird these transformative human rights education efforts in South Asia and beyond as BRAC has expanded globally to other parts of Asia and to sub-Saharan Africa (Bajaj 2012, 2017a; Bajaj, Cislaghi, & Mackie 2016; Flowers 2003; Smillie 2009; Tsolakis 2013).

The two cases of human rights education initiatives presented here have been selected for a variety of reasons in two domains: national context and organizational strategies. In terms of the national contexts of their work, the two nations occupy different sizes and locations in South Asia: India is the largest regional economy (yet still classified as a lower-middle-income country) with a population of 1.35 billion and an average literacy rate of 77 percent; Bangladesh is a low-income nation plagued by natural disasters (increasing in the wake of the climate crisis), with more than 160 million residents and an average literacy rate of 73 percent (UNICEF 2020; World Bank 2015). Further, while both countries have constitutional guarantees for the right to primary education, there is little in government policy requiring human rights education (Bajaj 2017a).

In terms of organizational strategies and the scope of their operations, People's Watch and BRAC offer points of similarity and difference that make putting their human rights education efforts in conversation fruitful. First, both People's Watch (India) and BRAC (Bangladesh) have a national scope of operations that transcend one particular region. Second, both have been the subject of scholarly attention to examine their approaches (Bajaj 2012, 2017a; Smillie 2009). Third, each case offers a different glimpse into transformative human rights education—the first is a three-year-long course in human rights for middle school-level children developed by an NGO that works in formal government-run schools; the second is a nonformal education program that utilizes "barefoot lawyers" to educate women through clear and accessible curriculum on their rights and how to access justice. Lastly, while there are over 2 million nongovernmental organizations in South Asia, and countless programs and movements using education to raise awareness about and transform social conditions, the two presented here explicitly call what they do "human rights education" (Bajaj 2017a). While this nomenclature is certainly not a measure of success or legitimacy, these two organizations were chosen because they provide insights into how those deliberately using the framework of human rights education are localizing it, making it contextually relevant, and reimagining its purpose and function in distinct locales (Bajaj 2017a).

From Sticks to Students' Rights: School-Based HRE in India

After attending the HRE training, I could understand the students from their point of view. For example, when I go to class, if I see a boy sleeping on the desk, I used to have the tendency to beat him or be harsh on him, without knowing if he may be hungry, without knowing anything about his family background. Maybe he is sleeping because he is having some problems in the family; maybe his father was drunk at night and beating his mother. So after attending this training, I have come to ask the children their problems instead of beating them; I try to understand the children, be friendly, and respect them. The students have started moving more freely and talking to me more also, so the distance [between us] is much reduced. If anything happens in their homes, if they have any family problems, they are sharing them with us. Even the District Education Officer has noticed these changes . . . because a lot of teachers have attended the training in human rights.

(HRE Teacher focus group, as cited in Bajaj 2012: 123)

People's Watch is a human rights organization founded in 1995 in the southern Indian state of Tamil Nadu. The organization has pioneered HRE in India nationwide through its Institute for Human Rights Education (IHRE), which has complemented the organization's legal and advocacy work (Bajaj 2017a). Starting as an experiment in a handful of schools, IHRE currently operates in 4,000 schools in more than eighteen states of India (Bajaj 2012). The organization has developed textbooks, delivered trainings for teachers, and expanded their human rights work (initially primarily on caste discrimination and police abuse) into a broad-based educational program. As connections were made with the United Nations Decade for Human Rights Education (1995–2004), IHRE was able to gain support by aligning with international efforts to promote human rights education and translating these interests into funding for their work (Bajaj 2017a).

Cooperation and collaboration with local government officials has also been essential since most of the 4,000 schools IHRE operates in are government-run (Bajaj 2012, 2017a). Textbooks have been developed in multiple regional languages, and more than 500,000 Indian students have participated thus far in a three-year course in human rights. Year one introduces students to human rights, year two focuses on children's rights, and year three addresses discrimination and inequality (Table 4.1).

IHRE's model aims to introduce students in primarily government schools and those from marginalized communities (those from the lowest castes, Indigenous groups, and others) to human rights concepts and principles. The course is taught by teachers from these schools who attend trainings to offer two human rights classes per week for three school years (grades six, seven, and eight). Teachers either volunteer to be their school's representative for this program or are assigned by their headmasters; in

Table 4.1 Content and Pedagogy of the IHRE Textbooks

Topics	Methods
(In order of frequency, from highest)	*(In order of frequency, from highest)*
1. Poverty/underdevelopment/class inequalities	1. Reflective/participatory in-class exercise
2. Gender discrimination/need for equal treatment	2. Illustrated dialogue or story
3. Child labor/children's rights	3. Community interviews and/ or investigation and research
4. Caste discrimination/untouchability/ need for equality	4. Small group work and discussion
5. Social movements/examples of leaders and activists	5. Creative artistic expression (drawing, poetry, etc.)
6. Religious intolerance/need for harmony and pluralism	6. Class presentation
7. Rights of Indigenous/Adivasi communities	7. Inquiry questions & essay writing
8. Rights of the disabled and mentally ill	8. Role play, dramatization, song-writing
9. Democracy	9. Letter writing to officials
10. Environmental rights	10. School or community campaign

From Bajaj 2012: 79.

practice, those attending the trainings tended to be teachers with a preexisting interest in the subject or younger teachers who were "volunteered" by their administrators.[2] Both male and female teachers were active human rights teachers in the IHRE program (for more information on the larger study, see Bajaj 2012).

Officials from the Institute of Human Rights Education maintained contact with teachers over the phone and through in-person visits; there were also refresher trainings and opportunities for human rights educators to get together throughout the school year sponsored by the organization. The textbooks developed by IHRE and trainings included concepts related to general human rights guarantees; corporal punishment and other forms of violence; children's rights; and issues of discrimination based on caste, gender, religion, ability, skin color, and ethnicity, among others (Bajaj 2017a).

After the HRE lessons began, many students reported (as in the quote at the beginning of this section) that teachers were more attentive to students' rights, particularly related to the outlawed but commonly utilized practice of corporal punishment. While students discussed attempting to intervene in social injustices they found in their communities, as discussed extensively elsewhere (Bajaj 2012), what were equally interesting were the responses that teachers had to learning about and teaching human rights.

While teachers are often discussed in human rights education literature as messengers who simply transmit human rights instruction, IHRE focuses on teachers as correspondingly important *agents* of human rights education who can go through transformative processes as well as take action, rooted in knowledge and skills, in their own lives as well as those of students and community members (Bajaj 2012). Many human rights abuses that take place in Indian government schools (which primarily serve relatively poor children)—including gender discrimination, caste discrimination, and corporal punishment—are often perpetuated by teachers or allowed to occur among students without any intervention. For example, respondents discussed multiple cases of teachers who verbally and physically abused students based on their caste backgrounds or poor academic performance and mentioned several examples of sexual abuse as well. Given teachers' relatively respected status in rural areas as part of a minority of literate professionals there, their potential transformation through human rights education as allies and advocates of human rights can result in effective interventions on behalf of victims, whether the victims are their students or not (Bajaj 2012, 2017a).

Human rights education created an opportunity for teachers to exert their agency in a large bureaucracy that often dehumanized both educators and students. A core part of the training on the HRE textbooks developed by People's Watch included participatory activities for students to identify and analyze human rights and social inequalities in their own communities. When teachers learned more about their students, and as students shared more with teachers perhaps with less fear of getting beaten, it allowed for close relationships to form. One teacher, Mr. Kumar, discussed buying prizes with his own money for students to speak publicly and sing songs about human rights at local festivals. He also talked about how the HRE program helped foster relationships in his classroom so that he began to see his students just like his own son who attended a nearby private school (Bajaj 2012, 2017a).

As teachers and students formed close-knit and reciprocal bonds, many came to see challenges in the community as a collective project for them to address. Numerous teachers interviewed discussed taking some form of action to address problems they saw in their lives, their communities, or those of the children and families (Bajaj 2012, 2017a). These examples ranged from trying to convince family members not to pull children out of school to work or not to marry off girls at a young age, to reporting abuse they learned about in schools and homes. Mr. Gopal, a teacher from the state of Tamil Nadu, related the following incident, emblematic of several other instances wherein teachers had reported an abuse:

> In the first year of human rights education, my student, Kuruvamma, overheard from a neighbor that if their child was born a girl, they would kill it since they already had three female children. The child was born a girl and what they planned to do was make the baby lie down on the ground without putting any bed sheets and put the pedestal fan on high speed in front of her. The baby can't live—she would not be able to breathe and then she would automatically die. Kuruvamma told me and together we gave a complaint in the police station. The family got scared and didn't kill the baby. Now that girl is even studying in first standard. My student Kuruvamma is now in high school. (as cited in Bajaj 2012: 127)

In many communities where the HRE program was offered, female infanticide was a common practice, although it is indeed illegal in India. It is estimated that more than 3 million girls have gone missing in India through sex-selective abortions (after a fetus is determined to be a girl) and infanticide, in poor and rich communities alike (The Hindu 2012). Students and teachers reported encountering evidence of infanticide, including young students happening upon dead (female) babies or overhearing stories such as the one earlier with Mr. Gopal and his student Kuruvamma (Bajaj 2012, 2017).

Of course, the introduction of HRE overlays existing socioeconomic realities, such as those that drive practices like infanticide. Even amid adverse material conditions, students identifying abuses—and having teachers willing to help report or intervene—were noted by both students and teachers as critical components of making human rights come alive. A key by-product of the transformative education offered by IHRE is that it gave meaning to the educational process by deeply engaging the educators (Bajaj 2012, 2017a). Mrs. Mohanta, a retired teacher from Orissa who taught human rights education for many years, continued going to the trainings and visiting her former school to help with classes even after her retirement given the satisfaction she derived from being involved.

While the IHRE program in India has been operating for more than two decades, upward of thirty-five years ago, a Bangladeshi NGO began offering nonformal education through trainers, known as the "barefoot lawyers." We take up in the next section how they seek to empower poor women who are unable to access justice.

"Barefoot lawyers" as Human Rights Educators in Bangladesh

BRAC's human rights and legal aid services programme is dedicated to protecting and promoting human rights of the poor and marginalised through legal empowerment. The blend of legal literacy initiatives with comprehensive legal aid services throughout the country helps spread awareness needed to mobilise communities to raise their voices against injustices, discrimination and exploitation—whether at the individual or collective level . . . Our "Barefoot Lawyers" impart legal literacy and spur sustainable social change by raising awareness and informing people of their rights. They operate on a 3P model of "Prevent-Protest-Protect" and are usually the initial contact points in their communities when human rights violations occur.

(BRAC, n.d.)

BRAC is the largest NGO focused on development in the world. It emerged just after Bangladesh's war for independence from Pakistan in 1971. The organization was founded by Fazle Hasan Abed as a relief organization, but now, in its fifth decade of operation, BRAC has programs in education, health, economic development, and women's empowerment across Bangladesh and internationally in various countries, such as Afghanistan, South Sudan, the Philippines and Uganda. In order to mitigate reliance on donor funding, BRAC—unlike most NGOs—also operates various income-generating enterprises such as a dairy business, handicraft stores, and a university (Smillie 2009). BRAC is referred to as the largest NGO because it has a staff of more than 100,000 people (mostly women) and the organization serves over 100 million people. Its nonformal education program has received commendation for its tremendous efficacy in providing culturally relevant and locally tailored education for marginalized children who lack access to government schools due to poverty; over 3 million children have been enrolled and the program boasts an extremely low dropout rate as compared to government education (Smillie 2009). While children are one group of recipients of BRAC's educational efforts, youth and women also receive education in their rights through the women's empowerment program (Bajaj 2017a).

BRAC's Human Rights and Legal Services (HRLS) program, started in 1985, has multiple components, of which human rights education is just one. In the school-based HRE example from India (discussed previously), students were taught about human rights, and action often ensued of their own accord or with teachers' help. In BRAC's program, action and redress for violations are central to the human rights and legal services program. According to BRAC, HRLS (1) provides "legal and human rights education and awareness to rural poor in particular women, and to local community leaders"; (2) provides "legal services, in particular alternative dispute resolution and court oriented legal aid"; and (3) "creates and activates social catalysts drawn from among the village elite to respond to human rights violations" (Islam et al. 2012: 6). Core to BRAC's approach is human rights education as the foundation for the legal, advocacy, and community mobilization strategies that build on top of this awareness for marginalized women (Bajaj 2017a).

Through the HRLS program, nonformal educators provide adolescent girls and women a foundational fourteen-day course as the first step in the program. The Human Rights and Legal Education (HRLE) course draws from the approaches in BRAC's other educational initiatives as well as the organization's original grounding in participatory approaches to development. For example, a report profiling the HRLS program noted that approaches included "workshops, committees, popular theater shows, and courtyard sessions to bring local leaders together and effectively engage the entire community in preventing and addressing human rights violations" (Kolisetty 2014: 41), similar to the popular education methodologies discussed in the previous chapter. A BRAC senior staff member noted that the pedagogical approach and curriculum are tailored to the realities of poor, rural women in Bangladesh: "This might be the only time we have access to this household or to this woman so we would like to have a sustainable impact on this person's life. One of the ways I believe we do that is by making the methodologies interactive in such a way that it becomes a personal journey rather than just a class" (interview, July 12, 2015, as cited in Bajaj 2017a).

As a result, the HRLE course starts with situating the learner in an analysis of their own lives the first few days and further offers basic knowledge about the legal system and human rights more broadly. The course—taught by *shebikas* also known as community paralegals or "barefoot lawyers" who advocate for people's rights in poor, rural areas—emphasizes laws related to common problems encountered by women, namely: dowry, mistreatment and abuse from spouses, child marriage, divorce, having no right to land and inheritance, among other topics (see Table 4.2). Since there are different laws in Bangladesh for individuals of different religions, these trainings also

Table 4.2 Content of HRLE Fourteen-Day Course

1	Myself and My Community
2	Family and Social Analysis
3	Social Discrimination and Gender
4	Abuse
5	Basic Rights and Entitlements
6	International Rights Mechanisms (CEDAW, UNCRC, UNCAT, etc.)
7	Marriage
8	Dowry
9	Divorce, separation, guardianship and custody, postnuptial rights
10	Police Duties and Jurisdiction
11	Hindu, Muslim, and Christian women's right to land
12	Opportunities for women to own and control land
13	Land mutation, tax and state-owned land
14	Closing

From BRAC, 2013 and from interview with BRAC staff member.

elucidate distinct rules and norms under the customary laws that apply to particular women related to the issues they face.

All of the training materials for the courses are pictorial given that many rural women are illiterate (women's literacy in Bangladesh is around 60 percent, and largely skewed toward urban women) (World Bank 2015). Many of the materials interrogate common gender stereotypes, utilizing drawings of real-life situations as a starting point (akin to Paulo Freire's approach of using a generative theme to spark discussion of broader injustices), as discussed in the previous chapter (Freire 1970).

After each fourteen-day course, the three most vocal and participatory women are selected to participate in the training to become *shebikas* or barefoot lawyers who help women access justice and also facilitate future trainings and courses. Ongoing training is provided both to participants in the fourteen-day courses, as well as trainers who undergo longer trainings and ongoing "refreshers" for professional development. BRAC notes, "The refreshers are an effective way of standardizing the quality of the *shebikas'* performance and of keeping them updated on current laws" (BRAC 2013: 55).

The HRLE course—as one piece of the larger HRLS program that includes education, legal aid services, and community mobilization—offers a holistic approach to addressing the challenges faced by poor, rural women in

Bangladesh. Many of them, unaware of their rights, are subject to abuses by husbands and corrupt officials who may accept bribes rather than enforcing laws that are meant to protect rural women. In reflecting on the overall vision of the HRLS program, a senior staff member of BRAC noted:

> We try to bring about a level of conscientization [related to] the inter-linkages between oneself and one's community and then the larger political structure. So instead of going into the law and the rights first, we start with a bit of a social analysis; understanding and asking questions and getting towards knowing one's own self and one's environment . . . What is very important is to understand the *agency* of the person. Most people are not aware of their own agency in their own lives. They feel like there's a predestined karma, like I was born to be poor or I was meant to die poor. But what if one can understand, *who am I really* apart from being the wife of so-and-so, or the mother of so-and-so? What do I want to do with my day, if not my life? (as cited in Bajaj 2017a: 227)

Agency and empowerment for poor, rural women are at the core of the human rights and legal education courses offered by BRAC. The entire design of the courses vis-à-vis structure, content, and pedagogy coupled with the mechanisms to allow women to seek justice offer a way to combat marginalization in a highly stratified social context (Bajaj 2017a). Transformative human rights education in this case includes knowledge of oneself and one's role in society in order to counter internalized forms of oppression that limit poor women from even believing they have rights. Once this social analysis is sparked, the women in BRAC's programs recognize their own inherent dignity and can find meaning, hope, and agency in the information about human rights that apply to all.

Discussion and Concluding Thoughts

In a region known for rote learning in schools and strict hierarchies—based on age, gender, class, and/or caste—transformative human rights education occurs in countless classrooms and community centers, spearheaded by innovative nongovernmental organizations. Policymakers in India and Bangladesh, while perhaps engaging in international discussions about the right to education and human rights education, are not, by and large, drawing on Freire's notions of empowerment and social transformation. Given that context, transformative human rights education espouses a "globalization from below" ethic where global ideas are taken up critically by grassroots organizations in that contested space. These ideas not only offer techniques and methods for inculcating critical consciousness about processes of exclusion but can also offer learners the chance to question unequal social relations. Both People's Watch and BRAC draw on these legacies in order to infuse their human rights education programs with meaning and relevance for the marginalized children, youth, and women who participate in them.

Facilitators and teachers in these programs, whether community- or school-based, are essential to the efficacy of teaching about rights because they are the primary catalysts for participants' transformation. Educators worldwide seek to offer students knowledge and skills to permit them to effectively respond to their current and future realities. In the case of the two examples offered earlier from South Asia, trainers and teachers draw from their own personal understandings of human rights to offer learners a chance to analyze and take action based on the social conditions that surround them. The issues relevant for these communities include ones such as gender violence, caste inequalities, discriminatory laws, child labor, communalism, and corruption.

Transformative human rights education in South Asia offers a way to draw upon the visions of Paulo Freire (1970) and South Asian social reformers such as Mohandas Gandhi (Bajaj 2010), Savitribai Phule, and Dr. B.R. Ambedkar to push learning spaces to move beyond mere laboratories for future citizenship toward sites that integrally embed opportunities for active participation in democratic life. Knowledge of human rights guarantees paired with students' ability to observe the gap between such legal promises and actual realities in their homes and neighborhoods can offer learners the chance to critically engage and advocate for justice in their communities (Bajaj 2017a).

This chapter has offered two examples of how human rights principles are translated into education for marginalized groups—whether Dalit children in India or semi-literate rural women in Bangladesh—in South Asia. Like the case studies in Chapter 2, these examples shed light on how global movements like peace and human rights education are applied in context, and offer insight into the ways that community-based organizations adapt and localize HRE meaningfully and appropriately to their settings. The next chapter explores the convergences between peace education and human rights education more deeply by focusing on and amplifying the intersections of the shared principles of transformative agency and dignity.

5

Bridging the Fields
Conceptualizing Dignity and Transformative Agency in Peace and Human Rights Education[1]

Chapter Outline

Centering Dignity in Liberatory Education   100
Conceptualizing Agency in Liberatory Education   104
Concluding Thoughts   112

The previous chapters of this book have outlined the histories, models, frameworks, and key developments in the fields of peace education and human rights education, as well as their application, respectively. This chapter situates concepts of dignity and transformative agency, as intertwined foundations of both fields, within larger theoretical bodies of literature to not only offer scholars and practitioners important insights for their engaged work, but also to thread the ways in which peace and human rights education overlap. While the previous chapters examined each field distinctly, this chapter explores more closely some of their intersections and brings in some analysis of another related field, that of social justice education, "the goal of [which] is to enable individuals to develop the critical analytical tools necessary to understand the structural features of oppression and their own socialization within oppressive systems," and "it also aims to connect analysis to action" (Bell & Adams 1997: 2). We place these three fields under the umbrella of "liberatory education" given their shared commitments to individual and collective transformation, justice, and liberation (for more on liberatory education, see the work of critical pedagogues such as Antonio Darder [2014], Paulo Freire [1970 & 2000], bell hooks [1994], Gloria Ladson-Billings and Henry [1980], and Peter McLaren [1996]).

In this chapter, we build on the tree with intertwined roots metaphor that was discussed in the Introduction. While the visual possibility tree generated by the undergraduate students (Figure I.2) shared earlier theorized their own vision of a world filled with peace, justice, and human rights, we posit in our book that dignity and agency form part of the same soil that nourishes the related fields of peace education and human rights education. We argue that these concepts mutually form part of the groundwork to justice-based, liberatory educational efforts generally, and devote much of this chapter to exploring the concepts of dignity and agency in educational research more broadly to show how they anchor these approaches. Returning to our conceptualization of the fields of peace and human rights education as one tree with intertwined roots, we have created our own visual, in the form of a banyan tree, to illustrate these shared underpinnings of the fields. While we have demonstrated the distinctions between the fields thus far in this book, here we hone in on the fertile terrain of their conceptual intersections.

As seen in Figure 5.1, the roots are the foundational concepts and include dignity and transformative agency (which we discuss in this chapter) as well as the broader concepts of justice, liberation, decolonization, antiracism, equity, Ubuntu (as discussed in Chapter 1), empathy, and solidarity. The large trunk of liberatory education has the fields of peace education, human rights education, and social justice education closely wrapped around it, with many overlaps and intersections among these fields. We have conceptualized the branches as the ways in which that learning takes place in these interrelated fields and included approaches such as dialogue, praxis, critical consciousness, culturally sustaining pedagogies (Paris & Alim 2017), reclaiming subjugated knowledges, and multiperspectivity. The leaves and fruits represent the broad outcomes that the fields espouse, such as positive peace, negative peace, community engagement, respect for human rights, planetary stewardship, and global citizenship. One of the unique features of banyan trees is their capacity to drop down new roots (which overtime conjoin and coalesce with the primary trunk). We argue that these new drop-down roots are the renewals of the field, spurred by its global spread and engagement by new scholars, reviving and building upon firm

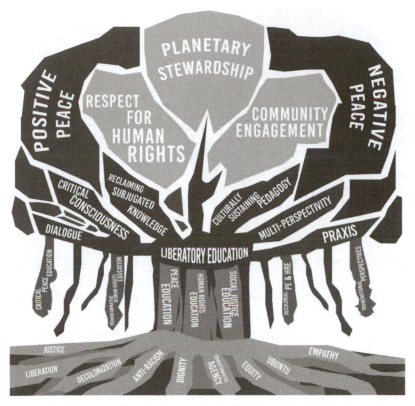

Figure 5.1 Educating for Peace and Human Rights Possibility Tree.

foundations and traditions in the spirit of reflexivity and growth. A few new directions in the image include critical peace education, transformative human rights education, decolonial approaches to peace and human rights education, and transrational perspectives; however, there may be and are more, and we have intentionally left some of the roots (as well as branches and leaves) blank to consider other possibilities.

Our previous chapters have explored peace education and human rights education in detail, and while we include social justice education here, given some if its commitments, we are unable to delve fully into this field in this book (for further conceptualizations of social justice education, see Bell & Adams 1997; Picower 2012). Building from the trunk of the tree of liberatory education to further define what such an endeavor is, Figure 5.2 demonstrates the common tenets of education for peace, human rights, and social justice that we place under the umbrella term of "liberatory education" (other educational projects such as ethnic studies and anti-racist education could be included as well). Furthermore, despite their key differences, peace

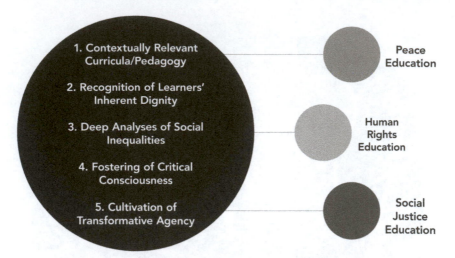

Figure 5.2 Shared Tenets of Liberatory Education (adapted from Bajaj 2018).

education, social justice education, and human rights education—in their more critical, transformative, and engaged forms—coalesce around the goal of honoring the inherent dignity of learners and fostering transformative agency in students; in turn, students develop the capacity to act in the face of structural constraints and advance individual and collective goals related to positive social change (Bajaj 2009, 2018; Bourdieu in Reay 2004; Hantzopoulos 2016; Solorzano & Delgado Bernal 2001). Figure 5.2 demonstrates the shared underlying commitments of peace education, human rights education, and social justice education despite different manifestations in distinct contexts.

As the figure highlights, the shared tenets of liberatory education, exemplified by peace education, human rights education, and social justice education, are the following:

1. **Contextually Relevant Curricula/Pedagogy**: Within liberatory education, learning materials, educational approaches, and pedagogical strategies are tailored to the learners' contexts and take into account historical trauma and ongoing violence that may impede the learning process. Such efforts must be "culturally sustaining" (Paris & Alim 2017) and sociopolitically relevant (Bajaj, Argenal, & Canlas 2017) in order to reach learners in meaningful ways.

2. **Recognition of Learners' Inherent Dignity**: Educators, administrators/leaders, and policies must honor the inherent dignity of learners and their families in the educational process (whether in formal, nonformal, or informal settings). Sylvia Wynter's (1994)

conceptions of "human-ness" highlight how marginalized groups have long been seen as less-than-human, and such beliefs often carry over into educational settings. Building on Wynter (2003) and Mignolo's (2000) notions of who gets to be seen as fully human, Zembylas notes that "only particular kinds of ethical subjects are recognizable as 'human,' while all others are excluded through [processes of] racialization and colonization" (2020). Honoring dignity requires acknowledging the humanness and inherent worth of all learners—and speaking back to the historical forces that have led to the dehumanization of some and the overvaluation of others[2]—as a foundation for liberatory learning.

3. **Deep Analyses of Social Inequalities**: Issues of power and inequality are explored in liberatory education to lead to deeper understandings of issues of privilege and marginalization as they are experienced differentially in local, (trans)national, and global contexts. Exploring social location allows for learners to situate themselves and analyze inequalities, their roots, and how they are positioned. Such analyses also offer possibilities for imagining and enacting solidarity.

4. **Fostering of Critical Consciousness**: Learners are able to analyze inequalities and arrive at complex understandings of issues. Critical consciousness, as conceptualized by Freire (1970), always has an eye toward action in his cycle of praxis, wherein knowledge leads to action, then reflection, and then new action in an iterative and ongoing process. Critical analyses of media and dominant modes of thinking are central to the fostering of an authentic critical consciousness as well (Jocson 2007).

5. **Cultivation of Transformative Agency**: As learners are engaging in praxis, they are also developing their ability to act in the face of inequities and injustices in ways that are relational, coalitional, strategic, and sustained (as will be discussed later in this chapter). Such lessons offer real-world applications of learning (the way educational thinkers such as John Dewey, Maria Montessori, Mohandas Gandhi, and Paulo Freire envisioned) and can offer learners lessons on participatory engagement in the present, and practice for future engaged democratic citizenship.

With these five underlying shared tenets of liberatory education identified, we now delve further into the two areas that most unite these fields: dignity and agency. We first start with a discussion of dignity and then follow with a conceptualization of agency in liberatory education.

Centering Dignity in Liberatory Education

The single most critical source of human rights is the consciousness of the peoples of the world, which have waged persistent struggles for decolonization and self-determination, against racial discrimination, gender-based aggression and discrimination, denial of access to basic minimum needs, environmental degradation and destruction, and systemic "benign neglect" of the disarticulated, disadvantaged, and dispossessed (including the Indigenous peoples of the earth). Thus, human rights cultures have long been in the making by the praxis of victims of violations, regardless of how rights are formulated, that is, regardless of the mode of production of human rights standards and instruments.

(Baxi 1997 as cited in Hantzopoulos 2016)

As noted by Indian legal scholar Upendra Baxi, approaches to liberatory education, particularly when promoted through peace and human rights education, require "serious engagement" with the histories of grassroots human rights movements; indeed, there must be an awareness of "a history of everyday moral heroism of diverse peoples asserting the most basic of all rights: the right to be human and remain human" (142–3). In many ways, this speaks to the underlying and generative principle that defines the enactment and purpose of peace and human rights education: *human dignity*. According to peace education scholar Betty Reardon (1996), this principle inherently links the numerous forms of rights and entitlements described in various peace and human rights documents and that may contextually vary across the globe.

The notion of dignity is the bedrock upon which the United Nations Universal Declaration of Human Rights (UDHR) rests and serves as a foundational principle for the entire international human rights framework. Scholars have argued that human rights are the ethical core of peace education (Al-Daraweesh & Snauwaert 2015; Reardon 1996), and that dignity, which is the foundation of human rights, undergirds the combined enterprise of peace and human rights education. As the UDHR asserts that there is an inherent dignity of all people, scholars of philosophy and ethics have parsed out the dimensions of dignity as put forth in the UDHR as a moral and legal framework:

The idea of inherent dignity is very closely connected with the *individual*; however, the implementation of laws on the rights, traditions and moral rules, may well also be connected with *collective* entities, and *group dignity* may well be detrimental to the dignity of the *individual*. In this way, the discussion on human rights is closely linked to the principle of dignity, and one may argue that the equal rights of all is the *practical outcome* of the dignity concept. In the UDHR, inherent dignity is indeed the presupposition on which the rights are built, and the reason why the rights should be legally protected. (Düwell et al. 2014: xix, *italics in original*)

At the time that the UDHR was adopted in 1948, less than a third of the nations that exist today were part of the newly formed United Nations, since the majority of the globe was still under colonial rule. While philosophers from all over the world crafted the Declaration, debates about collective rights and dignity have evolved in later international documents such as the United Nations Declaration on the Rights of Indigenous People, which states that "Indigenous peoples have the right to the full enjoyment, as a collective or as individuals, of all human rights and fundamental freedoms as recognized in the Universal Declaration of Human Rights" and that "Indigenous peoples have the right to the dignity and diversity of their cultures, traditions, histories and aspirations" (2007). Certainly, scholars such as Baxi (1997), Mignolo (2000), Wynter (2003) and many others would demand deeper interrogation of the "human" part in "human rights" in order to ensure the equal dignity of all peoples beyond the discursive level. A commitment to "decolonial ethics" for peace and human rights education can shift dignity from being part of the "liberal, multicultural or cosmopolitan ethics embedded in these fields" toward dignity as a praxis of being human, as Wynter (2003) would term it, and toward "taking an active stance against colonial patterns of hierarchization and oppression in peacebuilding and human rights efforts" (Zembylas 2020).

Critical and transformative approaches to peace and human rights education privilege the agency, experiences, struggles, and beliefs of the "learners" (both collectively and individually). Because they valorize learners as agentive actors in their own and their communities' social worlds, these approaches inherently place primacy on human dignity. While these approaches are generally found in grassroots and collective social movements, they can also be enacted in schooling contexts if there is a more radicalized reconception about the purposes of schooling.

When liberatory education moves beyond an emphasis on content and academic learning, there is much potential in viewing schools as sites of transformation and social change for the students who attend them (Hantzopoulos 2012; 2016). Particularly, when peace education, human rights education, and social justice education are attentive to both the localized experiences and knowledges of the students who attend these schools, as well as participatory processes, skills, and structures that may engage them in social action and change, they become not only sites for a more holistic form of liberatory education but also sites in which the humanity and dignity of school actors are centered in the school. When schools adopt this comprehensive view, they are transformed into sites that build more vibrant cultures of possibility for their students and pursue meaningful societal change writ-large. As such, the implementation of these forms of liberatory education necessarily embraces dialogical, problem-posing, and participatory/praxis methods; multiple, varied, and alternative viewpoints and content; and horizontal organizational structures that foster collaboration and connection rather than hierarchy and compartmentalization.

Critical pedagogy and democratic processes are at the heart of enacting liberatory forms of education and honoring learners' dignity (Hantzopoulos 2016). Grounded in concepts of justice and transformation, critical pedagogy engages teachers and students in the processes of recognizing and using their own experiences and knowledges as catalysts to transforming their lives and social worlds (Freire 1970). Coined "critical consciousness," these processes both call for a dialogical pedagogy among students and teachers and require that educational sites be inclusive, participatory, and democratic. The concept of democracy in particular is often met with skepticism because it is increasingly seen as a closed system that does not respond to people's basic needs (McGinn 1996); however, critical educators must respond to this skepticism by reclaiming the word, as something that is experienced and lived, moving beyond the "engineering of consent toward predetermined decisions [to a] . . . genuine attempt to honor the right of people to participate in making decisions that affect their lives" (Apple & Beane 2007: 9). If schools and nonformal educational settings endeavor to be sites in which *all actors* contribute to knowledge construction and decision-making, the fundamentals of more inclusive participation in a democracy can be both learned and practiced. In this way, democracy is not seen as stagnant but as something continually shifting and more of a "dynamic, striving, and collective movement than a static order of stationary status quo" (West 2004 as cited in Hantzopoulos 2016).

Liberatory education that draws from the traditions of critical pedagogy and democratic education mostly intersects with the critical forms of peace education and human rights education described earlier in this book. Since a holistic pedagogical approach rooted in dignity engages young people as actors in their own learning, attention to *process* resocializes students academically, and is, therefore, equally as important as the *product* of learning. Reardon (1996) and Zembylas (2011) map possibilities in connecting the two fields of peace education and human rights education, specifically by retheorizing certain taken-for-granted conceptualizations and practices that ground them. Reardon argues that the two forms of education are inseparable, particularly when all forms of violence (which are at the core of peace education as discussed in Chapter 1) are seen as an assault on human dignity (which is at the core of both peace education and human rights education). Zembylas (2011) also sees compatibility when human rights themselves are understood as ethical projects anchored in responsibility and empathy. This congruence rests in reconceptualizing human rights in direct relation to human suffering (rather than viewing them as context-specific entitlements or violations) and by encouraging praxis that ethically and contextually responds to that suffering (Hantzopoulos 2016). In turn, "this pedagogical praxis does not simply affirm rights uncritically; instead, it engages in a serious political analysis that recognizes the dilemmas and tensions involved, especially in post-conflict societies. [It] does not only focus on human rights violations but also unveils possibilities for solidarity and acknowledgement of common suffering with the other" (Zembylas 2011: 576).

The emphasis on human suffering need not be applied solely in what are seen as conflict or postconflict societies; in fact, one could argue that the legacies and histories that define the United States may warrant a similar reconceptualization. Even within schools, students endure humiliating policies that have denied them their dignity, as explained in Chapter 2. As Koenig (1997) states:

> Humiliation is the enemy of human dignity. Humiliation is a powerful experience, the impasse to being human. In defending our dignity, we refuse to be humiliated. We must recognize this in others. Unless we learn to live a life in which we do not degrade, disgrace, demean, or violate the dignity of the other on any level, personal, or communal, the cycle of violence, oppression, and abuse will go on ad infinitum. (Koenig 1997: xiv)

Yet, like human suffering, human dignity can frame both a conceptual and praxis-oriented approach, as it has remained elusive in the experience of marginalized youth in the United States and globally (Hantzopoulos 2016).

In highly unequal contexts where certain groups have faced centuries of violent domination, centering dignity in educational spaces humanizes the learning process and also serves as an important foundation for both educators and students. The companion of dignity is agency, something that is cultivated when dignity is honored, to catalyze transformative learning and action. While discussed earlier when referring to critical pedagogy and democratic processes, we tease out the dimensions of agency in the next section to hone in on its transformative aspects.

Conceptualizing Agency in Liberatory Education

The concept of "agency" lies at the core of many liberatory forms of education that draw from Paulo Freire's theories of education raising learners' critical consciousness and equipping them with the knowledge, skills, and networks to act for positive social change (Freire 1970), as explained in earlier sections. The term "agency" is utilized widely across disciplines to refer to a variety of behaviors and actions. This section theorizes the concept of *transformative agency* more deeply, since it lies at the center of educational projects, namely: peace education, human rights education, and social justice education (Bajaj 2018).

Agency and Resistance in Educational Research

Notions of student agency are central in resistance theories, which emerged from the theoretical propositions put forth in the 1970s onward through educational studies suggesting the multiplicity of ways in which students, teachers, parents, and communities can contest the process of social reproduction through schooling (Aronowitz & Giroux 1993; Foley 1991; MacLeod 1995; Weis 1996; Willis 1977). These theories countered the highly deterministic nature of reproduction theories that posited that socioeconomic class is reproduced generation after generation through public schooling (Althusser 1979; Anyon 1980; Bourdieu & Passeron 1977; Bowles & Gintis 1976). Sociological studies of student resistance in public schools in Europe and North America largely equated agency with opposition to dominant cultural discourses and practices that often resulted in "self-damnation" (Willis 1977: 3) or "self-defeating resistance that helps to recreate the oppressive conditions from which it originated" (Solorzano & Delgado Bernal 2001: 310). Building on these various conceptualizations, it is important to note that domination does not always result in opposition, that oppositional behavior is not always a form of resistance, and that not all forms of resistance are socially deviant (Bajaj 2009). Jeffrey (2012) notes that "young people's social practices [can be] simultaneously progressive and reactionary" (250). Agency and resistance are often used interchangeably and are complex when examined in educational contexts (Bajaj 2018).

In educational research, two groups of resistance emerge through ethnographies of schooling and examinations of social inequalities in education: (1) oppositional resistance (Bowles & Gintis 1976; Willis 1977), and (2) transformative/strategic resistance (Aronowitz & Giroux 1993; Giroux 1996, 1997; Solorzano & Delgado Bernal 2001). Scholars have asserted that individual consciousness and community resistance through collective action have some role to play in transforming schools from serving only the dominant class to serving the interests of other sectors in society as well (Apple 1982; Foley 1991; Freire 1970; Aronowitz & Giroux 1993; Noguera & Cannella 2006). Through the cultivation of an individual and collective consciousness based on a critique of social inequalities, belief in one's present or future agency may ensue (Bajaj 2009, 2018). Departing from traditional resistance theorists who see agency primarily as opposition (Willis 1977; MacLeod 1995), critical theorists assert that "the concept of resistance must have a revealing function that contains a critique of domination and provides theoretical opportunities for self-reflection and struggle in the interest of social and self-emancipation" (Aronowitz & Giroux 1993: 105). Further, Solorzano and Delgado Bernal define "transformational resistance" in contrast to oppositional or conformist forms of resistance by examining the collective action of Chicanx students in Southern California as "political, collective, conscious, and motivated by a sense that individual and social change is possible" (Solorzano & Delgado Bernal 2001: 320). Scholars Robinson and Ward (1991) refer to such collective consciousness raising and subsequent actions as "resistance for liberation" in their seminal work with adolescent African American youth.

Freire (1970) argued that education must heighten students' critical consciousness as they come to analyze their place in an unequal world and that resultant from this elevated critical consciousness is a transformative sense of agency that can lead to individual and social change (Bajaj 2009, 2018; Noguera, Cammarota, & Ginwright 2006; Giroux 1997; Hantzopoulos 2015, 2016a; Noguera 2003). Transformative agency can be fostered among students in various settings, and more recent empirical research in the United States and globally has identified such agency-enabling factors as participation in activist-oriented after-school programs (Bajaj, Canlas, & Argenal 2017; Kwon 2013), knowledge of and personal contact with those engaged in collective struggle (O'Connor 1997), and deliberate efforts to foster agency through school discourses and practices (Bajaj 2009, 2012, 2018; Hantzopoulos 2011, 2016a; Miron & Lauria 1998; Shah 2016).

Dimensions of Agency in Liberatory Education

This section explores how scholarship from different fields conceptualizes various dimensions of agency (Bajaj 2018). It also focuses on the potential pitfalls when seeking to cultivate the transformative agency of marginalized populations (children, youth, and adults) who face barriers—and sometimes, even violent backlash (Bajaj 2012)—in enacting the lessons learned in sheltered educational spaces that have alternative norms to those of the larger society. Conceptualizations of agency draw from French sociologist Pierre Bourdieu's theorizations of structure and agency; Bourdieu and Passeron (1977) argued that, through the reproductive mechanisms of schools and other social structures, individual subjectivity is produced to *align* with existing relations of power. As a result, students with more *social and cultural capital* are able to reproduce these privileges through schools that value the dispositions, tastes, and practices of dominant classes. Through the same process, marginalized students internalize their subordination through the *habitus*, "the set of common sense assumptions and embodied characteristics that are indelibly marked by such social factors as class, race, and gender" (Kennelly 2009: 260).

Anthropologists of education have built on Bourdieu's theories to define agency as the "inherent creativity of the human being given expression through subjectivities that both fashion and are fashioned by the structures they encounter" (Levinson et al. 2011: 116). Further, through forms of emancipatory or liberatory education, students can come to question the received wisdom about relations of power and, in turn, interrogate both the content they have learned and the processes through which marginalization occurs. Critical inquiry and engagement, which are at the core of peace, human rights, and social justice education, are inherently relational and contextual endeavors; and agency, empowerment, and resistance are often espoused as desired outcomes for learners (Bajaj 2018).

Bajaj (2018) has presented four dimensions of agency explored in scholarship from various fields to offer a framework to conceptualize transformative agency. In this model, transformative agency is constituted by (1) agency that is sustained across contexts and time; (2) agency that is relational and enacted with others; (3) agency that attends to the bounded-ness of peoples, histories, cultures, and contexts (Chavez & Griffin 2009); and (4) agency that is strategic with regard to analyses of power, long-term consequences, and appropriate forms of action. Taken together, these dimensions of agency can ultimately better equip learners to interrupt and transform unequal social conditions and, we argue, constitute the four necessary components of "transformative agency."

Component 1: *Sustained Agency*. Students are participating in an after-school program run by a community organization that explores social issues from a critical perspective. Through interactive pedagogy, critical inquiry, and the caring space cultivated by the facilitators, students develop a social action project to intervene in a local injustice. They come back to the space to reflect and plan further actions. Their collective agency has been fostered in a process that Paulo Freire referred to as the cycle of *praxis*, wherein theory spurs reflection, which spurs action and further reflection, as mentioned in the previous chapter (Freire 1970).

But, what happens to agency once cultivated? Many scholars have examined how youth in particular may exhibit agency while they are in educational programs where alternative social norms are valued (Bajaj 2009, 2018; Hantzopoulos 2015; Murphy-Graham 2009; Shah 2016), such as the hypothetical one mentioned earlier; once students leave, however, the pressures and norms of the larger society often result in a dissipation of the ability to act independently toward transforming unequal conditions (Kabeer 2002). Scholars have termed this "situational agency" (Bajaj 2009) or "thin agency" (Klocker 2007). Klocker, in her work on child domestic workers in Tanzania, defines "thick agency" as contingent upon "actors with varying and dynamic capacities for voluntary and willed actions" (85); this stands in contrast to marginalized children, youth, and adults whose ability to act is constrained ("thin agency") by "highly restrictive contexts" (85).

In scholarship in childhood studies and international education, various factors are discussed with regard to creating more sustained and "thick" agency. In her work on girls' schooling in India, Shah discusses education as a potential "thickener" of poor girls' agency; once educated, more options may exist for economic mobility and stronger marriage prospects in terms of girls entering families with potentially less violence and social restrictions on their freedom. Murphy-Graham (2009) similarly examines an educational program for young women in Honduras that expanded their understanding of gender inequities with a cohort of learners and cultivated their agency when considering their next steps. Hantzopoulos's (2015) work examines how young people in schools circumvent larger structural and systemic barriers when confronted with obstacles by paying attention to how they mediate and negotiate these tensions to their advantage in unexpected, unassuming, and contradictory ways. Other scholars have discussed extensions of the alternative space in which agency was first cultivated (e.g., in Bajaj's previous research in a school espousing peace education in Zambia and in a human rights education program in India) through alumni networks, opportunities for ongoing involvement, and mentorship from teachers and administrators (Bajaj 2009, 2012, 2018).

Sustained agency as a component of transformative agency within education for peace, human rights, and social justice requires attention to how educational spaces can prepare learners for transitions into other contexts where norms may be different, and create mechanisms for self-reflection, group insights, and shared problem-solving even beyond the protective educational setting (Bajaj 2018).

Component 2. *Relational Agency*. Relational, at its very basic definition, merely refers to the ways that humans are connected; when exploring *relational agency* vis-à-vis the larger conceptualization of transformative agency, this constitutive element establishes that individuals cultivate agency with others, in dialogue, and through interactions (Bajaj 2018). In her work in the field of feminist studies and in her research with young activists, Kennelly (2009) defines relational agency as

> the contingent and situated intersection between an individual's social position within a *field* of interactions, and the means by which the relationships within that field permit that individual to take actions that might otherwise be inconceivable—or, in other words, permit them to achieve a *habitus shift*. (264, *emphasis in original*)

In Kennelly's research, interactions with others fostered the development of agency within a subculture of activist young adults in urban centers in Canada.

In Shah's (2016) research in India, the relational components of agency— defined differently perhaps than Kennelly—sometimes created "thinner" forms of agency as girls had to weigh their further schooling alongside greater economic insecurity for their families and thus often dropped out or agreed to early marriages as a deliberate choice to improve the economic standing of their families. Deep connections to collective networks, such as families or ethnic groups, thus created pressure to not act solely for the individual good (even if the girl was part of an educational community seeking to collectively resist dominant gender norms), if it meant harm or disruption to their families. For Shah, *relational agency* means examining how rural Indian girls' agency is negotiated among members of a family, intergenerationally, and in concert with socioeconomic constraints.

White and Choudhury (2007) found through their research with street and working children in Dhaka, Bangladesh that "the influence of adults has been critical in shaping the form that children's agency has taken, through the particular kinds of 'supplements and extensions' they provide" (545). The authors found that the initial strategies the children developed, which were "deeply counter-cultural, a bulwark against the structural violence which underlay the daily violence and poverty in which the children lived," shifted through the adult facilitators' participation; facilitators, while providing necessary skills and prompts to the children for dialogue, did not share the children's "counter-cultural commitments" and led the children "increasingly to reflect a more mainstream set of values" (545). White and Choudhury's work on children's agency in the Global South demonstrates that while agency can be collective and relational, it may not necessarily always be transformative. Thus, the four components laid out in this chapter are required to work in tandem to guide the cultivation of agency toward its transformative potential (Bajaj 2018).

For peace, human rights, and social justice education, the component of relational agency is central for understanding the process of critical consciousness and the desire to act in the face of injustice. Interactions between educators and students, among students in their peer groups, and between students and their families/communities all constitute the basis through which relational agency develops and can incline toward transformative agency when combined with the other three components presented here.

Component 3. *Coalitional Agency*. Coalitional agency, as theorized by scholars Chavez and Griffin (2009), is by its very nature relational, or connected to others; but it is also about connections to larger histories, examinations of power asymmetries, and situating current interrogations within a larger trajectory of intergenerational activism and solidarity. "A coalitional agency implies that our ability to affect social change, to empower others and ourselves necessitates seeing people, history, and culture as inextricably bound to one another" (Chavez and Griffin 2009: 8).

While the framing of "coalitional agency" comes from feminist scholarship (Chavez & Griffin 2009), it has been applied to examining educational spaces in which Freirean pedagogies are being utilized to raise students' critical consciousness. In her study of a human rights education program for Dalit (formerly called "untouchable") and Adivasi (Indigenous) youth in India, Bajaj (2012), extends Chavez and Griffin's concept of coalitional agency to understand how students from different socioeconomic, caste, religious, and gender backgrounds worked together to intervene in injustices they witnessed in their communities (such as female infanticide, forced/early marriage, caste violence, and child labor). By seeing themselves as "bound to one another," students who had been learning about human rights through a three-year course—as discussed in Chapter 4—engaged in social action on behalf of others and worked together to promote human rights and alter unequal norms and social relations. In her study of Youth Space, a program in the US Midwest seeking to raise the critical race consciousness of African American youth, Dierker (2016) draws on Chavez and Griffin's concept of coalitional agency to find that youth agency "resides in connectedness" (31) and aided in the young adults' formation of a counternarrative to racial inequality (42).

Within education for peace, human rights, and social justice, coalitional agency represents a form of praxis that is defined by solidarity (Bajaj 2018). It is exemplified in the Indigenous Mayan phrase *In lak'ech*, translated as "You are my other me," and the Nguni Bantu word *Ubuntu*, translated as "I am because we are," as discussed in Chapter 1. These concepts align with philosopher Kwame Anthony Appiah's framing of a "rooted cosmopolitanism" that engages both the particular and the universal in situating individuals in a shared humanity (Appiah 2005). Such concepts involve a larger collective imagining in the process of understanding social inequalities and, in educational contexts, cultivate within learners a desire to collectively struggle against violence and inequality for the benefit of all. It can be summarized in the quote from Dr. Martin Luther King Jr.'s 1963 *Letter from a Birmingham Jail* that "Injustice anywhere is a threat to justice everywhere. We are caught in an inescapable network of mutuality, tied in a single garment of destiny. Whatever affects one directly, affects all indirectly." Thus, coalitional agency is an essential component of transformative agency as it provides a collective identity and a connection to a larger community of those working toward social justice and human rights, transcending the barriers of the school and the family, creating a new space for alliances across differences where rights and justice can be collectively fought for and won.

Component 4. *Strategic Agency*. Literature from various scholarly fields has examined the tactical and strategic agency of children and youth (Bajaj 2018). Tactics can be defined as "immediate responses to the vagaries of fluid events" distinguished from "orchestrated 'strategies' aimed at long-term change" (de Certeau 1984; Honwana 2002; Vigh 2006, as cited in Jeffrey 2012: 248–9). This differentiation between short- and long-term agency is particularly useful when examining situations of children and youth in conflict (Bajaj 2018). The inability to think beyond the present moment in which life and death are in the balance may constrain their choices and decision-making. For example, applying de Certeau's (1984) distinction between tactics and strategies to the agency of child soldiers in Angola and Mozambique, Honwana (2002) provides the following analyses in her anthropological study:

> Applying de Certeau's distinction, it seems that these young combatants exercised what could be called a "tactical agency" to maximize the circumstances created by the constraints of the military environment in which they were forced to operate. Many had no prospect of returning home after raiding and burning villages, killing defenseless civilians, and looting food convoys. This was the life they were constrained to live, both in the years of age when they were abducted from their families and initiated into violence and terror. In this sense they were conscious "tactical" agents who had to respond to the demands and pressures of their lives. The exercise of a "strategic" agency would imply a long-term consequence of seeing the results of their actions concretized in some form of political change, which does not seem to be the case for the majority of the child soldiers. (Honwana 2002: 291)

Given the limited options of child soldiers to kill or be killed, strategic agency may be impossible in certain situations like these.

Strategic agency in peace, human rights, and social justice education requires the possibility to engage in long-term thinking ideally in a collective space and the ability to engage in deep analyses of power relations in order to chart a path forward in light of constraints (Bajaj 2018). There may not always be simple ways for marginalized youth to "navigate plural, intersecting structures of power, including, for example, neoliberal economic change, governmental disciplinary regimes, and global hierarchies of educational capital" (Jeffrey 2012: 246); however, the undertaking of strategic and deliberate analyses of future action is a core component of transformative agency, as illustrated in Figure 5.3, along with the other three dimensions.

Figure 5.3 Core Components of Transformative Agency (from Bajaj 2018).

The four components of transformative agency discussed situate it as a foundational part of liberatory education efforts that seek to activate learners' consciousness and ability to act in the face of injustices (Bajaj 2018). While honoring dignity infuses the space of learning, transformative agency is cultivated within the learning space and extends out of it to impact the community and society at large. Together, dignity and agency nourish the roots of peace education and human rights education in order for them to accomplish their goals of inspiring individual and collective transformation.

Concluding Thoughts

Conceptualizing dignity and transformative agency in liberatory education projects offers a framework in which we can situate our work as educators for peace, human rights, and social justice. By distilling how a particular program may correspond with the dimensions of agency and dignity, we can better understand how its work contributes to a larger goal of preparing youth for more agentic futures where their opportunities are expanded. Much funding for school-based or cocurricular programs focuses on academic achievement, college readiness, risk reduction, and preparation for the labor force. "Grit" and "resilience" are fashionable terms in educational discourse, but this chapter has shown the importance and transformative potential of honoring the dignity of youth and offering them the ability to cultivate their own agency through critical analysis of power relations, collective civic engagement, and long-term strategic thinking for their future.

Educational programming that has a liberatory vision can include and better align its curriculum, pedagogy, structure, staffing, and practices to the dimensions discussed in this chapter (see also Hantzopoulos 2016a). Moreover, peace, human rights, and social justice education can begin at any age, and young people can develop capacities to explore systemic inequalities and violence and imagine alternate realities and ways of being early on in their lives. Courses and after-school programs related to social issues/action, the arts, leadership, sports, and ethnic studies are all areas that are well-suited for greater integration of the components of dignity and transformative agency. These approaches would enhance such programming in a more holistic manner.

Our single tree of peace and human rights education (see Figure 5.1), with its roots deeply intertwined, offers many possibilities for new visions and futures. In discussing a "decolonial ethics" for peace and human rights education, Zembylas offers a strong case for the "renewal" of these fields using the concept of the pluriverse attributed to "the Zapatistas' decolonial political vision of a world in which many worlds . . . coexist" (Mignolo 2018: ix):

> The "renewal" of HRE and PE, then, is inextricably linked to knowledge-production and cultivation as participation in practices that aim to make possible and viable the existence of new ethical relations with others and engage in ongoing struggles for decolonization. HRE and PE as knowledge practices are not isolated from decolonization efforts; on the contrary, to insist on renewing these fields, academically, ethically, politically, and practically means radical institutional, epistemic and ethical reforms that erase existing colonial remnants of knowledge in all manifestations of what is called HRE and PE. To enable this radical renewal of HRE and PE, then, our conceptualizations of "human rights" and "peace" as Western conceptions need to abandon their claim to universality and should be replaced by pluriversality. (Zembylas 2020)

In the departure from Eurocentric assumptions and default positions, peace and human rights education must unearth subjugated knowledges, continually regenerating our approaches in the fields.

In our research across different national contexts thus far, we have found the concepts of dignity and agency to offer a shared ground upon which liberatory educational projects can flourish. But as we decolonize the terrain of peace and human rights education, we cannot assume that these concepts will be universal. Engaged praxis will yield new ways of being and knowing. Dignity and agency are two (perhaps among many) shared commitments across peace, human rights, and social justice education, and this chapter offered further insights into the convergences and divergences of the histories, evolutions, and shared principles of the fields.

6

Concluding Thoughts and the Way Ahead

Chapter Outline

Key Contributions and Developments in Peace and
    Human Rights Education   118
Pressing Questions for the Field   120
Advice for Scholars, Students, and Practitioners   122
The Way Ahead   124
Conclusion   126

In this book, we have laid out the histories, models, and core tenets of the related fields of peace education and human rights education (HRE) that we envision as akin to a banyan tree whose divergent and distinct roots are deeply intertwined. We have also examined in greater depth what some of the principles of each of these fields look like in practice in places such as the United States, South Asia, and elsewhere. The previous chapters offered scholars, students, and practitioners a review of how the fields have developed, as well as conceptual frameworks to situate their research and practice in these fields, understanding the convergences and divergences among different perspectives and schools of thought in each field. In Chapter 5, we conceptualized how the shared commitments of dignity and transformative agency provide some of the nourishing soil to the intertwined roots of both peace education and human rights education.

In our previous scholarly work, we have collected global case studies of peace and human rights education in practice and sought to identify lessons learned across different regions, programs, and organizations that have engaged in critical, transformative, and/or postcolonial and decolonial approaches to peace and human rights education (for more information on these global cases, please see Bajaj & Hantzopoulos 2016). Across those case studies from sub-Saharan Africa, North America, Europe, South Asia, the Pacific Islands, the Middle East, and Latin America, we posited several lessons for the field of peace education that are extendable to the joint and intertwined fields of peace and human rights education discussed in this book. We have selected five of those lessons to share in an effort to bridge theory with empirical research that can inform praxis. These lessons include the following[1]:

(a) *The nature and process of peace and human rights education are relational, contextual, and situational, and not limited to the delineated roles of learner and teacher.* This builds on Freire's notions of dialogic learning and infuses the democratic and participatory vision of the learning process in critical and transformative liberatory education.

(b) *Normative and Eurocentric frameworks for understanding peace and human rights education must be interrogated and challenged across local and regional contexts.* The fields of peace and human rights education historically have been rooted in North America and Europe, where scholars have had more access to publishing and dissemination of their ideas through international mechanisms. Critical perspectives seek to uncover subjugated knowledge(s), challenge taken-for-granted truths, and illuminate wisdom from individuals and groups that have been historically silenced.

(c) *Intentions and outcomes must be integrated in peace education and human rights education; however, these concepts should be critically reflected upon before, during, and after the process of implementation.* Greater alignment is needed between good intentions and strong outcomes, which ought to be facilitated through critical, ongoing self-reflection on the part of curriculum designers and educators; program design should include regular and reciprocal dialogue with the participants in peace and human rights education initiatives.

(d) *Complex analyses of violence and power must undergird peace and human rights education efforts.* Related to the previous lesson, good intentions and outcomes result from rigorous analyses of both the root causes of problems, and the arrangements of power that contribute to violence and rights abuses in a given setting. The strength and possibility of peace and human rights education require that planners attend to the various vectors and forces of violence that impact teachers, learners, parents, and participants in a particular program, and that they include those voices in the design and implementation.

(e) *Examples of effective peace and human rights education can inspire other action in other places.* Successful models that are contextualized and relevant can offer important inspiration for other peace and human rights education efforts. As peace and human rights educators travel, share ideas, and disseminate findings of research through conferences, working groups, video conferences, and publications, good ideas resonate in different places, taking root in new ways. Identifying and describing these "pockets of hope" [de los Reyes and Patricia (2001)] offers counternarratives to dominant representations of conflict, inequality, and violence as entrenched and immutable.

With these lessons in mind (and many more that emerging and seasoned scholars can certainly add to the list), we hope that this new book series on peace and human rights education that this book launches will serve as a platform for debate and discussion among scholars, students, and practitioners to share research and perspectives on these fields, ultimately pushing them forward toward growth, renewal, and meaningful impact.

In developing this series, we, as coeditors of the new series and coauthors of this first book, invited leaders in the field to serve as members of our advisory board and we are delighted to have a group of nine expert advisers from across the globe.[2] For this final chapter, we interweave the advisory board members' perspectives with our own to shed light on frameworks developed and possible futures for the fields of peace education and human rights education. Some advisory members are rooted more centrally in the field of either peace education or human rights education, while others have worked at the intersections of these fields; as such, the responses may relate to one field specifically or both together. Beneath each topic are selected responses by advisory board members that demonstrate the diversity of perspectives on the fields of peace and human rights education. They share the many ways forward for scholars, students, and practitioners to pursue and carve out new pathways for the fields.[3] Walter Mignolo's (2018) recognition that multiple realities and worlds (human, natural, spiritual) coexist in time and space provides a lens through which to envision the multiple forms and directions that peace and human rights education can assume simultaneously.

Key Contributions and Developments in Peace and Human Rights Education

Pioneering human rights education advocate and one of the field's founding thinkers Nancy Flowers discusses the integral role of connecting HRE to social movements in the Global South as a lesson for scholars and practitioners globally. She offers:

> We all owe a great debt to Freire and our Latin American colleagues who showed us how human rights education could be an essential component of social change. The same for the Philippines. To take "education" out of the formal classroom and into the direct struggle for social justice was a major example and learning. I have also learned important lessons, both positive and negative, about how a generally conservative institution like a state school system can be used to ensure that rising generations have a global perspective of their rights as well a sense to responsibility to respect and preserve the rights of others everywhere (or not). The work of the Council of Europe has been an on-going learning example, even in their failures. (N Flowers 2020, personal communication, February 15)

With the perspective of decades of experience in human rights education specifically, having written several books and manuals for international organizations, Flowers identifies the importance of "taking education out of the formal classroom" for HRE and arguably for peace education as well. The link to social justice also requires that classrooms and communities have an opportunity to engage in critical sociopolitical analyses.

A seminal scholar in the field of peace studies/peace education, Asha Hans, former professor at Utkal University in India, acknowledges the important work that has been done to center feminist analyses of peace, conflict, and security by her and by collaborators such as pathbreaking peace education scholar Betty Reardon. She notes:

> In my writings and those of my contemporaries starting from Betty Reardon's *Sexism and the War System* (1996) to Cynthia Enloe's multiple writings on the subject of women and conflict, and Cynthia Cockburn's major work on women's networks in conflict areas, [we have] contributed to major feminist writings on conflict and peace, recognizing the ever-increasing militarism and its impact on women's and men's responses. Through this combined effort of peace research and learning, pedagogic practices in the field have

developed the theoretical basis of peace education. United Nations Security Council Resolution 1325 has provided a broad framework for peace at national and local levels and used by thousands of grassroots women usually as local action plans. The human security conceptual framework takes a broad comprehensive view of peace. The recent dimension of peace included in the human security framework is patriarchy, which provides the social insight and can contribute to the pedagogy of peace education. Peace education has developed in this context as a social value and, when defined from a human rights perspective, it includes the rights of people in all dimensions of life. (A Hans 2020, personal communication, February 25)

The foundation of a human security framework that centers feminist analyses of inequality, violence, and patriarchy allows for the development of peace and human rights education that is rooted in deep understandings of history, sociopolitics, and local context.

Writing as a leading scholar who often bridges peace and human rights education in his work, Professor Michalinos Zembylas, from the Open University of Cyprus, builds on Nancy Flowers' identification of the critical stance in recent years of the fields as a key development, stating:

I think that a key intellectual contribution by several of us in recent years is a deeper and more critical theorization of peace education and human rights education (hence the terms "critical peace education" and "critical human rights education"). For a long time, there has been a rather uncritical approach that simply praised the value of peace and human rights (education) without engaging with their multiple complexities, tensions, and paradoxes, as those are manifested in different contexts around the world (hence, ethnographic and in-depth case studies are really important). This has been gradually changing by acknowledging how peace/human rights are inextricably linked with power structures, social, and gender inequalities, and coloniality; these linkages are manifested differently in different contexts. The educational implications of acknowledging these complexities, tensions and paradoxes are immense and change the landscape of doing work in the fields of peace education and human rights education. (M Zembylas 2020, personal communication, January 30)

Zembylas acknowledges the shifts toward interrogating and diving into the "complexities, tensions, and paradoxes" that exist at the core of peace education and human rights education efforts and analyses. Such examinations ultimately can contribute to appropriately tailoring peace and human rights education over time to be more efficacious and responsive.

Pressing Questions for the Field

Given these insights, there are several considerations within and beyond this book that will continue to help us think anew about the distinctions, intersections, and critical directions of the fields. In this section, we combine some of the key questions that we (our advisory board and us, as editors) have identified for those in the fields of peace and human rights education. Notably, all of the questions pertain in some way to moving peace education and human rights education toward their critical, transformative, and decolonial iterations with increasing relevance for communities on the ground. We have attributed the questions to their authors, as many questions build off one another.

Asha Hans

(a) What do we mean by democracy in the context of developing countries and specifically related to economic and social equality?

(b) How do we need to unpack and problematize the location in which women are positioned in peace education, which has been creating segregation and stereotyping?

(c) How do we prevent violence, negotiate peace, boost economic recovery, and protect populations in conflict situations?

(d) In terms of peace education methodology, it is very important that we interrogate how to disengage gender from the binary framework.

Michalinos Zembylas

What are the limitations, tensions, and paradoxes that emerge when postcolonial/decolonial thinking is put in conversation with critical peace education/critical human rights education? What new theoretical openings emerge? What does this mean in educational practice? What new opportunities for transformative praxis emerge?

Nancy Flowers

(a) How can human rights education encourage critical analysis, challenge injustice, and question power and policies and still be part of/collaborative with governmental structures like public schools and human rights commissions?

(b) How do we address challenges that human rights education is "neo-colonial," Western, manipulative, and rejective of cultural norms of nondominant peoples? Are rights really "universal"?

Margo Okazawa-Rey

(a) How do we get folks—including ourselves—to envisage possibilities and visions of a just and peaceful world? Vision is the least articulated aspect of our work; we articulate lots of what we are against.

(b) How do we incorporate meaningfully feminist, transnational frameworks into the work?

(c) [How do we cultivate] a deeper understanding of power from intersectional, feminist, and materialist frameworks?

Monisha Bajaj and Maria Hantzopoulos[4]

(a) In what ways can the core competencies of critical peace education (namely, critical thinking and analysis; empathy and solidarity; individual and coalitional agency; participatory and democratic engagement; education and communication strategies; conflict transformation skills; and ongoing reflective practice) be further developed, expanded, and operationalized in practice? (Bajaj 2015).

(b) How do learners in different settings understand and act upon the insights drawn from pedagogies of resistance and critical/transformative/decolonial peace and human rights education in ways that are locally meaningful? (Bajaj 2015).

(c) How do the macro-cultural, political, and economic forces and institutions that shape one's quotidian existence inform the ways that peace and human rights education programs are contextually conceptualized? (Hantzopoulos & Bajaj 2016).

(d) How might scholars and practitioners rethink their efforts to engage in peace and human rights education research and praxis by resisting the totalizing and universalizing aspects of the field and considering the primacy of localized realities? (Hantzopoulos & Bajaj 2016).

These questions cull the thinking of leading scholars in the fields of peace and human rights education and, while certainly not prescriptive, the questions offer possible starting points for future research and grounded praxis that attend to the developments and trajectories of these fields. The in-depth annotated bibliography at the end of this book also offers readers a chance to chart their location in the fields and consider where their contributions may fit in to the efforts to develop and advance these fields.

Advice for Scholars, Students, and Practitioners

We also posed a question to leaders in the fields of peace and human rights education related to offering advice for scholars, students, and practitioners who may be already steeped in the fields or new entrants. Their advice ranged from conceptual to practice-related, and reflects their deep knowledge and experience with peace and human rights education in the Global North and Global South.

For instance, Nancy Flowers offers pragmatic insights. She states:

(a) Human rights education is a new field. Avoid reaching rigid definitions and conclusions. And it is a necessarily multi-disciplinary field. Be open to what you can learn from other disciplines, communities, activists, and people engaged with issues you know little or nothing about. HRE can be part of so many endeavors. Learn to look for the human rights dimension of every issue;

(b) Never cease to learn, especially from those whom you are "teaching";

(c) Look for allies in other fields, communities, and countries. (Flowers 2020, personal communication, February 15)

Staying open to learning—from other fields, from one's students, from the larger fields of human rights and human rights education—is central to Flowers' advice to others to be able to approach HRE with intellectual curiosity and cultural humility.

Similarly, longtime feminist peace researcher Asha Hans encourages us to incorporate continuingly more sophisticated and nuanced analyses into our work. She advises:

(a) Listen to women at the grassroots, especially the peace builders, about gender equality and inclusive peace. This will help build new concepts and frameworks.

(b) Gender is visualized as a binary in peace education, especially in the understanding of [different] cultures. This brings up issues of methodological implications in peace education. The male/female binary is narrow and do not get us the in-depth understanding unless we see women with multiple identities and locations.

(c) The lens of intersectionality in the discipline of peace education as a critical enquiry and critical praxis may be missing. The exploration of feminist engagements by tracing journeys—through narratives and feminist constructions of a subject-centered view of patriarchy—[should] be attempted.

(d) Above all, we need to analyze limits and possibilities in the localization of peace education and human rights education in diverse contexts. (A Hans 2020, personal communication, February 25)

Complexity and intersectionality infuse most of the advice from senior scholars about how to engage with our diverse fields in increasingly complex times, where inequalities are rising and crises expose vectors of protracted conflict, climate emergencies, global pandemics, widening education disparities, and overall increasing precarity.

Michalinos Zembylas offers his advice for newer scholars as well. He encourages scholars "to break new theoretical territories by trying to bridge the gaps between the fields of peace education and human rights education." Further, he states:

These fields are remnants of western epistemologies of coloniality and several approaches to peace and human rights are in fact perpetuating these legacies. These disciplinary and other boundaries exist partly because scholars are complicit by legitimating such boundaries, practices, or "territories" so to speak. Therefore, what is needed is a de-territorialization of these fields by breaking the traditional borders of "Now, I am doing peace education" or "Now, I am doing human rights education" and start thinking and doing peace *and* human rights as they are embedded in everyday life—outside disciplinary (or other) boxes. (M Zembylas 2020, personal communication, January 30)

In Zembylas' conceptualization, he notes the limitations of discursive disciplinary boundaries that ultimately contribute to reproducing some of the trappings of the normative foundations of the fields, as articulated in the previous chapters. The metaphor of the tree with intertwined roots is one way to build on this analysis and reconceptualize new terrain and possibilities for the fields. As the fields develop over time and become enjoined and grow together, the insights and analyses of both fields nourish and sustain the branches. We envision a banyan tree, one that sprouts roots in different directions and is made sturdy by a strongly grounded, yet sinewy, trunk.

The Way Ahead

Finally, building on the pressing questions and advice offered by leading scholars in both fields, we offer insights on the way ahead for the fields of peace and human rights education. The advice from our advisory board members fell into the broader categories of "advice for scholars" and "advice for engaged practitioners" in classrooms and communities, understanding that these roles also overlap.

Margo Okazawa-Rey, a renowned expert on militarism, gender, and conflict as well as a founding member of the legendary Black feminist Combahee River Collective in the 1970s, offers the following path forward for our fields, stating we need to engage in "visioning, solidarity/coalition work, and practices of peace-making rooted in realities of specific regions and types of conflicts" (M Okazawa-Rey 2020, personal communication, February 25). She further states that we need to "connect the dots between struggles, analysis, and identities" and "move away from identities as the cornerstone of organizing and towards understanding the current situation/ political moment" (M Okazawa-Rey 2020, personal communication, February 25).

Nancy Flowers offers similar visions of the way forward specifically for the field of human rights education. "Until educators of all kinds—especially K-12 classroom teachers and administrators—feel comfortable, inspired, and personally know and embrace human rights, the field will never extend to rising generations. I long to see knowledge of human rights as a prerequisite for obtaining a teaching credential, and teachers respectively need to be grounded in the United Nations Convention on the Rights of the Child." She further offers that "human rights should be part of the education of every public official, from the police officer on the beat to the elected office holder. The same is true for professional education, e.g., physicians, lawyers, social workers" (N Flowers 2020, personal communication, February 15). Integrating human rights education into every level of the education system has been part of Nancy Flowers' work for decades, and, as such, this aspiration continues in her vision for the way forward.

In the realm of scholarship in both peace education and human rights education, advisory board members see the way ahead converging with their previously stated advice to scholars, students, and practitioners in the field related to topics, approaches, and methodologies. Asha Hans, for example, argues that we need to develop new concepts and methodologies in peace education related to (1) Feminist analyses of political economy; migrants and refugees' struggles to cope with new types of extreme violence; (2) Learnings related to the enabling power of financing for peace, women's place at peace negotiations at all levels, participation in countering violent extremism; (3) Understanding the market and increasing poverty, climate change, the military, and its impact on environment, deforestation, etc.; (4) Using new methodologies of teaching in the classroom (e.g., social media, arts, dialogue, youth, intergenerational dialogue, constitutional rights); and (5) Bridging divides across communities by initiating new avenues for dialogues. (A Hans 2020, personal communication, February 2020)

Hans endorses a transformative vision for peace education and rigorous research that explores deepened societal understandings of power, place, politics, and participation. Hans also sees the inherent link to the field of human rights, stating that peace education "must include all of humanity and be based on dignity and equal access to basic needs/resources" (A Hans 2020, personal communication, February 2020).

Michalinos Zembylas' work explores the intersections of peace and human rights education particularly in contested contexts such as divided Cyprus. His vision of the way ahead for the fields reflects his scholarly contributions and further expands the critical and transformative forms of peace and human rights education.

I hope to see scholars bringing theoretical concepts and ideas from postcolonial/decolonial studies, feminist studies, new materialism, affect theory, and other theories to "look" at peace and human rights through new lenses. I hope to see work that is more critical of peace and human rights education and their consequences in everyday life. Work that takes into consideration sociological, feminist, and political theories to do that, not only psychological and cognitive ones—the dominant theoretical frames in the field of education for the past 100 years. (M Zembylas 2020, personal communication, January 30)

In the advice of senior scholars and their visions for the way ahead, there is a convergence around the need to learn from other fields and engage with decolonial, feminist, and other critical approaches to interrogate the normative assumptions and frameworks of peace and human rights education. The more robust conceptual engagement with the fields, and corresponding methodological and empirical rigor, can certainly yield new insights and propel the fields forward in their relevance and responsiveness to the contemporary challenges we face locally, transnationally, and globally.

Conclusion

Throughout this book, we have charted key moments, principles, and the institutionalization of the fields of peace education and human rights education respectively; we have also conceptualized where these fields intersect and are bound together by intertwined roots that are nourished by the undergirding concepts of dignity and transformative agency, among others. In this chapter, we have laid out where we go from here, highlighting possible research directions, key questions, and advice from scholars and practitioners with decades of experience and deep expertise.

This book has offered the metaphor and heuristic of the banyan tree to explain some of the shared roots of peace and human rights education, as well as their uniqueness as fields. As authors of this book and editors of the new book series on peace and human rights education, we reflect back on how we each first found refuge and inspiration in justice-based educational efforts as educators in formal and nonformal settings decades ago. We hope that this book offers scholars, students, and practitioners in the fields of peace education and human rights education—and the joint field of peace and human rights education, for which many of us advocate—similar refuge, insight, and inspiration. We hope that it stimulates more critical research and engaged praxis that will advance the field(s), as well as move our classrooms and communities toward greater peace, justice, and dignity for all.

Appendix

Annotated List of Further Reading in Peace and Human Rights Education[1]

Al-Daraweesh, F., & Snauwaert, D. (2015), *Human rights education beyond universalism and relativism: A relational hermeneutic for global justice*. New York: Palgrave Macmillan.

In *Human Rights Education Beyond Universalism and Relativism*, Al-Daraweesh and Snauwaert present a human rights epistemology that transcends the enduring tension between moral universalism and cultural relativism. A "free-standing normative universalism" is presented as such an epistemology—one that overcomes the universalism-relativism tension through "cross-cultural overlapping consensus" (34–44). Al-Daraweesh and Snauwaert draw from many existing conceptual frameworks to propose a new framework that is hermeneutic and culturally sensitive for future work toward global justice.

Andreopoulos, George J., & Claude, Richard P. (1997), *Human rights education for the twenty-first century*. Philadelphia: University of Pennsylvania Press.

This book serves as a resource for those educating, training, organizing, studying, and raising awareness of human rights education (HRE). With contributions from a diverse group of experienced activists, educators, and members of international organizations, *Human Rights Education for the Twenty-First Century* provides theories and concrete approaches to creating spaces for people to learn about their own human rights. Many different approaches are presented for various contexts—formal, nonformal, and informal—in which HRE may be implemented.

Andrzejewski, J., Baltodano, M., & Symcos, L. (2009), *Social justice, peace, and environmental education: Transformative standards*. New York: Routledge.

Written for researchers and educators, this book explores the linkages among social justice, peace education, and environmental education with several provocative essays that explore the concepts and practices of transformative education. Editors and authors discuss the standards movement to critique power, domination, and oppression; they envision liberation and the right for all humans, species, and ecosystems on the planet to live and prosper. Inspired by the Alaska Standards for Culturally Responsive Schools, chapters include examination of Indigenous cultural standards, human rights education, environmental education, and social justice education through the framework of transformative standards.

Bajaj, M. (Ed.). (2008), *Encyclopedia of peace education*. Charlotte, NC: Information Age Publishing.

The *Encyclopedia of Peace Education* emerged from a desire to create a living and democratic space for those involved in peace education from across the globe to contribute. As such, there are currently fifty entries that comprise the online Encyclopedia (https://www.tc.columbia.edu/epe/). In 2008, the editor decided to publish some of the entries as a classroom resource for peace education courses and the book includes guiding discussion questions, a glossary, as well as an introduction. The edited book seeks to serve as a "peace education primer" for college- and graduate-level students to understand the historical emergence, philosophical underpinnings, foundational concepts, and new directions in the field. The book seeks to answer the question "What is peace education?" in accessible yet not simplistic terms. The online encyclopedia offers free download of existing entries.

Bajaj, M. (2012), *Schooling for social change: The rise and impact of human rights education in India*. New York: Bloomsbury.

Schooling for Social Change presents multiple understandings of human rights education (HRE) through an examination of the Institute of Human Rights Education (IHRE), a nongovernmental program implemented in thousands of schools in India. The book is anchored in three essential arguments: that HRE includes a diverse array of initiatives whose outcomes depend significantly on the ideologies and populations involved; that, in the work to expand HRE, strategy is as important as pedagogy and content; and that social location affects capacity for change and the ultimate impact of HRE. Through extensive interviews and fieldwork in India, Bajaj traces the implementation and effects of education reform in India over the past several decades and complicates presumptions about what HRE looks like in practice.

Bajaj, M. (Ed.) (2017), *Human rights education: Theory, research, praxis.* Philadelphia: University of Pennsylvania Press.

This edited collection presents examples of HRE research and praxis from around the globe through in-depth chapters by leading scholars in the field. Examples are from given classrooms and communities in Asia, sub-Saharan Africa, Latin America, the Middle East, North America and Europe. An afterword by Nancy Flowers weaves together the contributions of the different authors writing from distinct disciplinary backgrounds.

Bajaj, M., Cislaghi, B., & Mackie, G. (2016), *Advancing transformative human rights education.* Cambridge: Open Book Publishers.

This text, an appendix to the "Report of the Global Citizenship Commission," gives a thorough illustration of transformative human rights education (THRED). The authors begin with a brief history of HRE and THRED as defined by various UN agencies, providing context for the principles and practice of THRED. Six principles of THRED are synthesized by the authors to help make meaning of the case studies presented—studies of formal and informal implementations of THRED in India, rural Senegal, urban Colombia, and Europe. This work promotes the use of the transformative model of HRE and does so with clear proposals for future activism by government and non-governmental organizations for human rights.

Bajaj, M., & Hantzopoulos, M. (Eds.). (2016), *Peace education: International perspectives.* New York: Bloomsbury.

This book brings together international perspectives of peace education scholars and educators to create an understanding of peace education that is grounded in the lived experiences of its practitioners. Acknowledging the great potential as well as the difficulties in practicing peace education— especially in conflict and postconflict societies—the contributing authors offer both theoretical and practical tools to students and teachers alike. Readers are given a guideline that inspires peace education as a critical practice—one that is particularly relevant in the current global context.

Bekerman, Z., & Zembylas, M. (2012), *Teaching contested narratives: Identity, memory and reconciliation in peace education and beyond*. Cambridge: Cambridge University Press.

In this book, the authors consider the influence of identity and memory on classroom practices and contexts. They critique the construction of Western psychologized notions of peace and reconciliation and how these have permeated the field of peace education by romanticizing notions of peace rather than understanding their complexities and multiplicity of understandings. The authors unpack concepts of culture, reconciliation, and collective memory, exploring how classroom practices exist amid contested narratives that are often imparted in nondialogical ways. Bekerman and Zembylas explore how power and the "politics of emotion" (115) are ingrained in teaching contested narratives, creating differential pulls toward individual emotions and collective belonging. The authors argue for reconciliation pedagogies that acknowledge power asymmetries, resist the pull toward closure, and delink (to the extent possible) from nationalist discourses. Bekerman and Zembylas conclude with a recommendation for teachers and students to become "critical design experts" in schools, (a) considering the importance of context, (b) "disrupting taken for granted assumptions about peace education" (189), and (c) "recognizing the power of emotion" (191).

Bekerman, Z., and McGlynn, C. (Eds.). (2007), *Addressing ethnic conflict through peace education: International perspectives*. New York: Palgrave Macmillan.

&

McGlynn, C., Bekerman, Z., Zembylas, M., & Gallagher, T. (Eds.). (2009), *Peace education in conflict and post-conflict societies: Comparative perspectives*. New York: Palgrave Macmillan.

&

McGlynn, C., Zembylas, M., & Bekerman, Z. (2013), *Integrated education in conflicted societies*. New York: Palgrave Macmillan.

These three volumes bring together comparative perspectives on peace education in conflict settings across the globe. Drawing lessons from distinct contexts, the volumes examine coexistence camps, integrated schools, and university-level peace initiatives from diverse locales, such as Israel, Cyprus, Northern Ireland, the Balkans, the Dominican Republic, Burundi, and South Africa. Taken together, the volumes offer insights into the challenges to and possibilities for peace education programs and policies that seek to mitigate ethnic tensions and promote reconciliation in postconflict settings. Taken individually, each book hones in on specific aspects of comparative work and the understandings they generate across contexts of the limits and possibilities of peace education in conflict settings. The editors of these books have advanced theoretical understandings of the dynamic role of peace education amid contested histories and protracted conflict.

Bey, T., & Turner, G. (1996), *Making school a place of peace*. Thousand Oaks, CA: Corwin Press.

Written for teachers at all levels, this book aims to combat the increasing levels of violence found in schools with a peace-oriented pedagogy. Emphasizing conflict resolution, social problem solving, and peacemaking skills, the authors suggest ways in which teachers can encourage productive social skills in students and promote a more peaceful school environment. The authors further outline the ways in which peace education can be best incorporated in curriculum, relationships with parents/families, as well as school-community partnerships. In terms of curriculum, the authors heavily emphasize the need for multicultural peace education to further establish understanding and tolerance necessary for peaceful conflict resolution.

Brantmeier, E., Jing, L., & Miller, J. (2011), *Spirituality, religion, and peace education*. Charlotte, NC: Information Age Publishing.

Written for educators, students, and researchers, this book explores education for inner and interpersonal peace through various religious and wisdom traditions: Confucianism, Judaism, Islam/Sufism, Christianity, Quakerism, Hinduism, Tibetan Buddhism, and Indigenous spirituality. It also explores wisdom traditions rooted in inner exploration, the development of skills, and contemplative practices in Part II of the book. A range of topics are explored: Daoism and narrative inquiry; 12 Step Programs for Peace; Gandhi, deep ecology, and multicultural teacher education; and wisdom-based learning in teacher education. Cultural awareness and understanding are fostered through an exploration by authors who are practitioners of the various traditions they write about.

Burns, R., & Aspeslagh, R. (1996), *Three decades of peace education around the world*. New York: Garland Publishing.

Drawing from the rich and dynamic discussion among peace educators of the Peace Education Commission of the International Peace Research Association, this anthology synthesizes the decades of peace education from international and comparative perspectives. Included chapters cover topics such as peace education in the context of war and peace, the role of peace education in global development, peace education as a form of resistance, complicated peace research ethics, and many more. Case studies are drawn from a wide range of international locales, from Poland to Japan to Africa.

Cabezudo, A., & Reardon, B. (2002), *Learning to abolish war: Teaching toward a culture of peace*. New York: Hague Appeal for Peace.

A peace education resource packet written for teachers, researchers, and activists at all levels, *Learning to Abolish War* is a comprehensive three-book anthology of peace education resources. The first book in the collection is on rationale for and approaches to peace education, outlining the central theoretical tenets of peace education as well as the key pedagogies for effective peace education. The second book consists of sample learning units concerning topics such as the roots of war/culture of peace, international human rights/institutions, conflict studies, and human security for students at all levels, from elementary to secondary. The third book includes tools and resources to sustain peace education activism, offering networking tools for organizations and online resources for educators.

Cannon, S. G. (2011), *Think, care, act: Teaching for a peaceful future*. Charlotte, NC: Information Age Publishing.

Written for educators, this book blends theory and practice to establish usable peace education praxis for educators. The central argument of this reflective book is that teachers should advance the causes of peace education in their classrooms to promote a more secure world based on justice and human rights through consciousness raising, caring, and engaging in action toward change. The author utilizes an empowerment model and provides ample practical ideas for teaching peace at the primary, middle, and secondary levels. Chapter topics include critical thinking, media literacy, critical imagining, school safety, literature for empathy development, creating local and global caring communities, engaged citizenship projects, student governance, debate, Model UN, and other social action projects. Chapters contain a plethora of photographs that illustrate concepts and practices in action. The book includes a very helpful appendix that includes an annotated bibliography of resources for both teachers and students. There is also a list of picture books for peace and global awareness.

Cargas, S. (2019), *Human rights education: Forging an academic discipline.* Philadelphia: University of Pennsylvania Press.

Sarita Cargas makes a case for an academic discipline in human rights that can and should be adapted to local contexts, contemporary issues, and the needs of faculty and students. Her call for the adoption of critical pedagogy has the potential to impact significantly how human rights is taught in the United States. Cargas identifies an informal consensus on the epistemological foundations of human rights, including familiarity with human rights law; knowledge of major actors including the United Nations, governments, NGOs, and multinational corporations; and, most crucially, awareness and advocacy of the rights and freedoms detailed in the articles of the UDHR. The second half of the book offers practical recommendations for creating a human rights major or designing courses at the university level in the United States.

Carter, C. (Ed.). (2010), *Conflict resolution and peace education: Transformations across disciplines.* New York: Palgrave Macmillan.

This edited volume explores interdisciplinary approaches to conflict transformation and offers in-depth case studies of how individuals are seeking to implement strategies in diverse locales. This edited volume emphasizes practice—exploring models in law, psychology, sociology, and education from the United States, the Philippines, India, and elsewhere. The book offers a diversity of perspectives, critiques of Western assumptions, and utilizes conflict analysis in examining structural violence in addition to direct violence.

Cislaghi, B., Gillespie, D., & Mackie, G. (2016), *Values deliberations and collective action: Community empowerment in rural senegal.* New York: Palgrave Macmillan.

In this book, the authors describe their study of a particular type of collective action in rural Senegal: values deliberations. Under Tostan's approach to community empowerment, values deliberations are meetings in which participants reflect together on local values, goals, and experiences and discuss ways to study and realize human rights. This book explains what values deliberations look like in practice and show how these sustained meetings lead to improvements in education, health, gender equality, and other aspects of the community. With first hand accounts from participants, the authors show how values deliberations enhance collective and individual agency, particularly for women, and ultimately help in the revision of unequal gender norms.

Cole, E. (Ed.). (1999), *Teaching the violent past: History education and reconciliation*. Lanham, MD: Rowman and Littlefield.

A collection of nine case studies using history education to promote tolerance and reconciliation, *Teaching the Violent Past* unites critical peace education perspectives from all over the world, ranging from Japan to Ireland. The edited volume is divided up into three parts. The first concerns the challenges of long-term reconciliation in history education, drawing from case studies in postconflict areas such as Germany, Japan, and Canada. The second is about reconciliation in process, where teaching conflict and tolerance in history is an ongoing process, drawing from Northern Ireland, Spain, and Guatemala. The third section is about peace education efforts that are challenged and/or jeopardized in Russia, Korea, and India/Pakistan.

Coysh, J. (2017), *Human rights education and the politics of knowledge*. London: Routledge.

Responding to the dominant discourse of human rights education—namely, the one that is developed by the UN and carried out by NGOs—this book asks critical questions about the power dynamics at play in HRE. Coysh highlights the complexity of both human rights and education theory and explains how these diverse ideas have been reduced to one dominant framework. She then advocates for a more radical practice of HRE: one that, instead of attempting to teach students the language of "universal" human rights, engages students in critical inquiry of oppressive power structures and their role in maintaining the status quo. Based in field research with NGOs working in Tanzanian communities, Coysh provides a thorough analysis of existing HRE programs and presents a strong case for the necessity of critical pedagogy in educational practice and policy.

DelFelice, C., Karako, A., & Wisler, A. (2015), *Peace education evaluation: Learning from experience and exploring prospects*. Charlotte, NC: IAP.

This timely volume looks at the fraught nature of educational evaluation tools for peace education programs and proposes frameworks that are more aligned with the goals of peace education. It fills an important gap as there has been very little written about peace education evaluation. The volume offers critical reflection on theoretical and methodological issues regarding evaluation in peace education programming and investigates existing quantitative, qualitative, and mixed methods evaluation practices of peace educators in order to identify what needs related to evaluation persist among practitioners. The volume shares practical examples of program evaluation across contexts, to inspire ways for practitioners and programs to consider new innovations and approaches.

Duckworth, C. (2014), *9/11 and collective memory in US classrooms: Teaching about terror*. New York: Routledge.

Drawing from extensive quantitative and qualitative data on how US middle and high school educators teach about the terrorist attacks of September 2001 in the United States, Duckworth offers a powerful look at the production of collective memory in US classrooms. The author argues that the events of September 11, 2001, have become a "chosen trauma" for the United States, examining the narratives offered (or absence of them) by educators. Key insights emerge about the "post-9/11 generation" and how young people are socialized into perspectives about nation, citizenship, and foreign policy in relation to perceptions of victimhood, conflict, and peace globally.

Edge, K. (Ed.). (2019), *Transnational perspectives on democracy, citizenship, human rights and peace education*. London: Bloomsbury Academic.

This anthology stresses the importance of transnational collaborations in democracy, citizenship, human rights, and peace education, especially in an increasingly globalized world. Globalization, it is argued, has involved advancements in technology as well as shifting political and economic relations—all of which necessitates rethinking current approaches to education. Through policy investigations, research data, and case studies, the contributing authors assert that transnational collaboration not only is crucial for building understanding of theoretical concepts, but could create practical relationships of accountability between national education systems. The book is divided into four parts: (1) Introduction, which contextualizes the need for transnational collaborations in a world of increasing mobility; (2) Transnational Perspectives on Democracy and Education; (3) Transnational Perspectives on Citizenship and Education; and (4) Transnational Perspectives on Peacebuilding and Human Rights Education.

Eisler, R., & Miller, R. (Eds.). (2004), *Educating for a culture of peace*. New York: Heineman.

In this edited volume concerning peace education, Eisler and Miller collected a variety of essays highlighting best practices in incorporating peaceful language, emphasizing social justice, and developing students' visions of peace. The authors argue that to counter the dominant culture of violence, educators everywhere must provide their students the tools to transform their relationships and environments through compassion, tolerance, and comfort in diversity. Through the essays, the authors provide a strong rationale for such a peace-oriented education and grounded approaches of incorporating peace-minded practices in everyday pedagogy and lesson plans.

Finley, L. (2011), *Building a peaceful society: Creative integration of peace education*. Charlotte, NC: Information Age Publishing.

Written for educators who work outside the classroom in the US criminal justice system, social services, or other social institutions, this book fundamentally critiques models that are rampant in these arenas. The central argument is that peace education must address both structural and institutional violence by questioning models and transforming them into partnership models governed by creativity, collaboration, and cooperation. The book is arranged as a critique and a call to action.

Flowers, N. (2000), *The human rights education handbook: Effective practices for learning, action, and change: Human rights education series, topic book*. Minnesota, MN: Human Rights Resource Center, University of Minnesota.

Conveying the "common language of humanity" is the whole purpose of human rights education. Concerned citizens need to understand and embrace the fundamental principles of human dignity and equality, and accept the personal responsibility to defend the rights of all people. This handbook is intended to help people who care about human rights to become effective educators, able to share both their passion and their knowledge. To further human rights education in its many forms, the handbook lays out the basics: why, for whom, what, where, who, and how. It draws on the experience of educators and organizations, illustrating their effective practices and distilling their accumulated insights. The handbook is designed to be used as a ready reference and tool: easy to read, easy to use, easy to photocopy. Each chapter can stand alone.

Galtung, J., & Udayakumar, S. P. (2011), *More than a curriculum: Education for peace and development*. Charlotte, NC: Information Age Publishing.

Using critical case studies of alternative peace education schools and projects, Galtung and Udayakumar explore how to best incorporate peace education in schooling practices. The authors examine structural practices that discourage or facilitate peace education through a study of successful and unsuccessful peace education efforts. Instead of an emphasis on peace education as a form of curriculum, the authors emphasize the necessity of educators "embodying peace" to truly produce a transformative peace-oriented educational experience. Education for peace and tolerance for the authors is "more than a curriculum"; rather, it is a lifelong process, both at the individual and collective levels.

Gaudelli, B. (2016), *Global citizenship education*. New York: Routledge.

In *Global Citizenship Education*, Gaudelli calls on educators to recognize the importance of preparing students to live in a more globalized and fragile world. This book offers both theory and practical illustrations of how global citizenship education (GCE) is implemented around the world—not just in elite schools but in historically marginalized communities. Gaudelli provides a comprehensive overview of GCE and adds student voices to realize the educational practice as it is functioning. Combining topics like sustainability and cultural diversity, this book creates a sense of urgency in the work to create educational systems that are inclusive and globally expansive.

Gerber, P. (2013), *Understanding human rights: Educational challenges for the future*. Cheltenham: Edward Elgar Publishing Limited.

In *Understanding Human Rights*, Gerber offers a legal scholar's perspective in the field of HRE policy. Gerber provides an analysis of the UN's efforts to support HRE over the past sixty years, pointing out deficiencies and making suggestions for future implementations. The UN's use of HRE as a tool to prevent human rights abuses is strongly supported, placing particular importance on improving the UN's recent activities and expanding recognition of HRE as an effective methodology.

Gevinson, S., Hammond, D., & Thompson, P. (2006), *Increase the peace: A program for ending school violence*. Portsmouth, NH: Heinemann Press.

Written for middle and high school educators, this book and accompanying videos provide practical lessons to walk students through the tangled emotional responses and potential for positive change encountered in conflict situations in schools. Student and community member interviews and real-world role-playing scenarios invite teachers to engage their students in skill development that hopefully will end and prevent various forms of violence prevalent in US schools today.

Hanna, H. (2019), *Young people's rights in the citizenship education classroom*. Cham: Palgrave Macmillan.

Testing the "universality" of international human rights frameworks regarding education, this book compares two deeply divided societies that are not often compared—Northern Ireland and Israel. In these two areas, Hanna looks closely at the practice of citizenship education in the context of societies in conflict, specifically highlighting how education rights are interpreted in various ways. From extensive qualitative research in Northern Ireland and Israel, Hanna synthesizes the interpretations of education rights into three common themes: representation of minorities in the curriculum, addressing difference through pedagogy, and preparing youth to live in divided societies. Throughout the book, Hanna complicates the work of citizenship education by highlighting the challenges of not only transferring international frameworks to a divided national context but transferring national frameworks to an individual school context. These challenges culminate in the final proposal that conflict societies embrace multiple "interpretive communities"—constituted of the different parties involved in interpreting education rights—to make citizenship education truly adaptable to local contexts.

Hantzopoulos, M. (2016), *Restoring dignity in public schools: Human rights education in action*. New York: Teachers College Press.

Restoring Dignity in Public Schools shares a hopeful counternarrative to the mainstream portrayal of distressed urban public schools in the United States. Drawing on ethnographic research with Humanities Preparatory Academy in New York City, Hantzopoulos examines human rights education (HRE) in practice and highlights the ways in which a culture of dignity, respect, and tolerance can be fostered in public schools. This book defines the elements of HRE practices and provides a grounded framework from which school leaders can find inspiration and ultimately build schools where students are encouraged to interact critically and creatively with the world around them.

Harmat, G. (2019), *Intersectional pedagogy: Creative education practices for gender and peace work*. London: Routledge.

Written for educators and researchers of peace education and academia at large, this book presents an intersectional approach to more equitable education. Halmat takes particular care to address the importance of language accessibility, beginning with a chapter about names and the way we tend to frame conflict. She then looks at peace education and human rights advocacy through the lens of gender identity, highlighting that critical awareness of gender is necessary to prepare younger generations to promote sustainable peace and justice in a quickly changing world. Throughout the book, Harmat discusses several recent and current human rights debates, including global migration crises and sexual violence campaigns such as #MeToo. This book is a timely response to a worldwide struggle to make sense of human rights issues and peace educators' role within that struggle.

Harris, I. (2013), *Peace education from the grassroots*. Charlotte, NC: Information Age Publishing.

This book presents voices of everyday peace educators from around the globe working to improve the lives of children and families. *Peace Education from the Grassroots* "tells the stories of concerned citizens, teachers, and grassroots peace activists who have struggled to counteract high levels of violence by teaching about the sources for violence and strategies for peace." Chapters come from different countries—Belgium, Canada, El Salvador, Germany, India, Jamaica, Japan, Mexico, the Philippines, South Korea, Spain, Uganda, and the United States. This book offers a cross-section of peace education practice on the ground.

Harris, I., & Morrison, M. L. (2014), *Peace education* (3rd edn.). Jefferson, NC: McFarland Inc.

This classic book in peace education, first published in 1988, deals with historical and religious trends/events that have shaped our understanding of peace, applications of peace education in the classroom, and implications of the use of peace education for students, schools, and communities. The book provides an in-depth overview of the constantly changing conceptualization of peace and best practices in peace education curriculum and pedagogy (in schools, churches, and other community spaces).

Harris, I., & Shuster, A. (Eds.). (2006), *Global directory of peace studies and conflict resolution programs* (6th edn.). San Francisco, CA: Peace and Justice Studies Association.

This compilation features perhaps the most comprehensive annotated guide to peace studies and conflict resolution programs at colleges and universities worldwide. The directory features programs at undergraduate, masters, and doctoral levels in over forty countries and thirty-eight states in the United States. Within the volume, the programs are described through their philosophy and goals, contact information, location, religious affiliation, and type of degree. Journals that publish peace and conflict studies material are also part of the volume. A more recent version of the searchable directory was updated and placed online at: https://www.peace-ed-campaign.org/view/peace-education-directory-study-peace-ed/

Holland, T., & Martin, J. P. (2014), *Human rights education and peacebuilding*. New York: Routledge.

Written in response to the lack of attention paid to human rights knowledge and skill building within postconflict settings, *Human Rights Education and Peacebuilding* demonstrates how HRE practices can help peacebuilding efforts in such areas. Chapter by chapter, this book analyzes the implementation of HRE in seven different postconflict contexts. For each area, the particularities of the local context are explored and the authors show how this context affects the rationale for and impacts of HRE programs. In this grounded examination, Holland and Martin shed light on both the challenges and the potential in using HRE as part of community peacebuilding in the aftermath of conflict.

Howlett, C., & Harris, I. (2010). *Books, Not Bombs: Teaching Peace Since the Dawn of the Republic*. Charlotte, NC: Information Age Publishing.

Written for educators, researchers, and students, *Books, Not Bombs* aims to explore the origins and evolution of peace education both inside and outside the classroom. Howlett and Harris are different from other scholars who generally focus on conflict resolution and peace pedagogy. Instead, they study peace education through the lens of opposing war and promoting social justice. In essence, this book provides a historical perspective of the development of peace education from the eighteenth century to the current day.

Howlett, C., & Lieberman, R. (2008), *For the people: A documentary history of the struggle for peace and justice in the United States*. Charlotte, NC: Information Age Publishing.

A historical docu-text, *For the People* provides secondary school students a comprehensive understanding of peace politics and activism from the eighteenth through twenty-first centuries. Through a historical perspective, Howlett and Lieberman weave in the story of the peace movement, its linkages to wider social justice movements, and its transformation from an advocacy for an absence of war to a push for equality for all. This book includes primary source documents, photographs, analyses, questions, and a list of references for students to conduct research of their own departing from this book. *For the People* is supposed to act as a supplementary guide to *A History of the American Peace Movement from Colonial Times to the Present*, written by the same authors.

Iram, Y., Wahrman, H., & Gross, Z. (Eds.). (2006), *Educating toward a culture of peace*. Charlotte, NC: Information Age Press.

This book was produced as a result of an international conference held in 2003 at Bar Ilan University in Israel. Many international perspectives are included, including those from Canada, Chile, Croatia, Germany, Mauritius, the Netherlands, the United States, Palestine, Israel, Australia, India, Jordan, and Morocco. This book tackles the critical issue of developing educational practices for a culture of peace. Major sections include peace education paradigms, globalization and peace, culture of peace perceptions, religiosity and culture of peace, and peace education initiatives.

Katz, S., & Spero, A. (2015), *Bringing human rights education to US classrooms: Exemplary models from elementary grades to university*. New York: Palgrave Macmillan.

Valuable for students and educators at all levels of schooling, this book provides ten models for successfully integrating HRE in the classroom. With a diverse selection of model projects, Katz and Spero examine a wide range of ages—elementary students to university students—and show that human rights education is indeed relevant to the United States, particularly to communities of color. Each of the ten projects is presented with discussion of its rationale, scope, challenges, and student responses, building an inspiring body of research that connects theory and practice in the promotion of HRE.

Keet, A., & Zembylas, M. (Eds.). (2019), *Critical human rights, citizenship, and democracy education: Entanglements and regenerations*. London: Bloomsbury.

Written for researchers, educators, and activists in a wide range of fields, this book provides an international collection of academic work centered on human rights, democracy, and citizenship education. The contributing authors take various approaches to the subject—including theory and case studies—but all present a critical view of the categories of human rights, democracy, and citizenship. Taken together, these works complicate existing categories and propose educational praxis that is more effectively justice-oriented.

Keet, A., & Zembylas, M. (2019), *Critical human rights education: Advancing social-justice-oriented educational praxes*. Cham: Springer.

In *Critical Human Rights Education*, Zembylas and Keet create space to rethink the theories and practices that have become commonplace in the field of human rights education. Honoring the critical approach they promote, the authors raise questions about presumed "truths" of human rights and open up the conversation toward renewal and change. Most of the chapters in this book were formerly published but are "reworked here in an effort to gain a deeper understanding of our ongoing struggles and concerns with theorising and enacting *critical* formulations of HRE" (1, emphasis in original). This book is a timely call to reexamine whether HRE praxes are truly social-justice-oriented and make space for the consistent change necessitated by critical pedagogies and practices.

Kester, K. (2020), *The United Nations and higher education: Peacebuilding, social justice, and global cooperation for the 21st century*. Charlotte, NC: Information Age Press.

This new book looks critically at the role of the UN's role in higher education, particularly on how its policies and curricula at one higher education institution unintentionally undermine the goals of local peacebuilding efforts. Drawing from the fields of educational philosophy and sociology, Kester not only theoretically unravels the undergirding premises that frame these initiatives but also considers new ways forward for peacebuilding and peace education.

Kingston, L. N. (Ed.) (2018), *Human rights in higher education: Institutional, classroom, and community approaches to teaching social justice*. Cham: Palgrave Macmillan.

This book brings together a variety of authors who consider how human rights education might be used to create "human rights campuses" in higher educational institutions. Together, the chapters illustrate that "HRE in higher education requires the intersection of three complementary approaches centering on institutions, classrooms, and communities" (2). Attention is given to several aspects of HRE that are especially relevant to higher education, including just administrative practices and collaborative research between faculty and students. It is stressed, however, that human rights discourse in higher education must extend beyond the boundaries of a single institution's campus. Case studies are presented of HRE as practiced in the broader community, such as teaching critical pedagogy to aspiring police officers, opening up dialogue at academic conferences, and contributing to the work of social justice-oriented organizations. This book expands and reframes current conceptions of HRE and shows that it is not just an option but a necessity that larger communities be involved in HRE for higher education.

Lantieri, L., & Patti, J. (1996), *Waging peace in our schools*. Boston: Beacon Press.

Written for educators, this book provides a foundation for a new vision of education based on teaching peace and creating peaceable classrooms. Focused on teaching conflict resolution skills and creative inclusive schooling environments that value diversity and cultural competence, the chapters explore the possibilities of peace pedagogy, mediation in schools, and peace in our communities. This book is hopeful and provides some needed approaches to promoting positive peace in schools.

Lin, J., Brantmeier, E., & Bruhn, C. (Eds.). (2008), *Transforming education for peace*. Charlotte, NC: Information Age Publishing.

In this edited volume, Lin, Brantmeier, and Bruhn bring together a myriad of voices and perspectives on peace education across national and social contexts. Case studies range from the study of actual classrooms to websites, from the US Midwest to Israel/Palestine, India, and Costa Rica. The authors attempt to (re)define and (re)conceptualize peace education in its own space. The book aims to use its diverse range of case studies to build a framework through which peace education can be a major educational paradigm. Written for educators and researchers at all levels, the book aims to be a resource through which effective peace education can be implemented effectively and studied/researched in more depth.

Magendzo, K., Duenas, C., Flowers, N., & Jordan, N. (Eds.). (2016), *Towards a just society: The personal journeys of human rights educators*. University of Minnesota Human Rights Center.

In the volume *Towards a Just Society*, twenty-five educators from around the world respond to the question, How and why did you commit yourself to human rights education? These highly personal narratives recount the diverse ideological perspectives and life experiences that have shaped their work in human rights education. Despite the diversity of experiences and realities, these testimonies offer much insight about the commonalities and differences that bind the field. This collection is highly accessible and readable and should be widely read by those interested in human rights education.

McCarthy, C. (2002), *I'd rather teach peace*. Maryknoll, NY: Orbis Books.

In this book, McCarthy, a longtime *Washington Post* columnist, chronicles one semester teaching peace at six schools. These schools varied from higher education institutions to public high schools to youth centers. In his curriculum, he employs tenets of peace education, such as nonviolence, pacifism/tolerance, and conflict management, and introduces key figures in peace activism, such as Mahatma Gandhi, Cesar Chavez, and Martin Luther King, Jr. The book aims to outline the ways in which McCarthy motivates students to explore issues related to peace, drawing from his teaching experiences in vastly different contexts.

Mirra, C. (2008), *United States foreign policy and the prospects for peace education*. New York: McFarland.

Carl Mirra explores the correlation between militarism in US foreign policy and peace education. The author situates peace education practices amid larger narratives and constructions of peace and war amid patriotism and international relations. Mirra looks at US foreign policy in historical perspective, critiquing the Cold War policies of free market expansion through multinational corporations at the cost of a genuine concern for human security. He argues for nonviolence as an ethic that should underpin US foreign policy. Mirra discusses the International Criminal Court as peace educator in that it holds the promise for a democratic and universal standard-bearer despite the United States' unwillingness to adhere to its jurisdiction. The author ultimately argues for nonviolence as a core value and "suggests that a holistic cosmology of humility and empathy can refashion the United States' role in the world" (138).

Noddings, N. (2011), *Peace education: How we come to love and hate war*. Cambridge: Cambridge University Press.

In this book, well-known educational philosopher Nel Noddings, most recognized for her theories on caring in schools, offers perspectives on how education can combat cultures of violence. Her primary focus is on "direct violence," such as aggression, war, and militarism, and little of the book is devoted to analyses of structural or cultural forms of violence. Nonetheless, the book provides a depth of perspectives on the psychology of war and the historical and cultural glorification of masculinity. Focusing on the United States, Noddings further discusses the differences between patriotism and cosmopolitanism, arguing that the former can lead to educational systems fostering hatred in times of war. She also discusses pacifism, war, and peace movements, arguing that women's experiences and values need to contribute to larger visions and conceptions of peace.

Osler, A. (2016), *Human rights and schooling: An ethical framework for teaching for social justice*. New York: Teachers College Press.

Human Rights and Schooling adds to the growing body of work regarding social justice in schooling, specifically making an important connection between international human rights standards and grassroots activism. Osler shows how existing human rights frameworks—namely, the UN Convention on the Rights of the Child and the Universal Declaration on Human Rights Education and Training—can support the work to realize justice in and through education. With examples from schools across the world, Osler discusses and complicates concepts such as cosmopolitan citizenship and intersectionality and shows how these concepts are used in practice to build solidarity within struggles for human rights.

Osler, A., & Starkey, H. (2010), *Teachers and human rights education*. London: Trentham Books.

This book serves as a useful overview of human rights education as practiced in classrooms. Osler and Starkey take the commonly used term "human rights" and show its real relevance in schools around the globe, building a more clear definition of what HRE seeks to do. Specifically, the principles of human rights are presented by the authors as foundational for creating learning spaces (and societies at large) where diversity and democracy can thrive. Thus examples of individual school environments centered on human rights are connected to students' engagement with larger efforts to promote justice and peace.

Page, J. (2008), *Peace education: Exploring ethical and philosophical foundations*. Charlotte, NC: Information Age Publishing.

The philosophical foundations of peace education have long been assumed and left unquestioned. In this book, Page investigates the various ethico-philosophical approaches to peace education. He argues that the philosophical underpinnings of peace education include: (1) virtue ethics, where peace may be interpreted as a virtue and/or vice versa; (2) consequentialist ethics, whereby peace education may be interpreted as education regarding the consequences of our action and inaction; (3) conservative political ethics, whereby peace education emphasizes the importance of the evolution of social institutions and the importance of ordered and lawful social change; (4) aesthetic ethics, whereby peace is understood as beautiful and valuable in itself; and (5) the ethics of care, whereby peace education emphasizes the value of trust and engagement with others. Throughout his book, Page addresses the history of these traditions, their strengths and the weaknesses, and the ways in which these traditions support peace education.

Palaiologou, N., & Zembylas, M. (Eds.). (2018), *Human rights and citizenship education: An intercultural perspective*. Cambridge: Cambridge Scholars.

Highlighting the interdependent relationships between human rights, citizenship, and intercultural education, Palaiologou and Zembylas present possibilities for education to promote "the values of freedom, tolerance, and non-discrimination" (2). Together, the chapters acknowledge the incompatibilities between some conceptualizations of human rights, citizenship, and multiculturalism and point to ways in which each can draw on the others. Theory, pedagogy, and policy are explored at various levels of education systems and in various regions. This book comes at an important time—one of growing migration crises and shifting discourse on citizenship and human rights. It encourages all of those working in education and policy to consider new ways of preparing students to become global citizens.

Reardon, B., & Hans, A. (Eds.). (2019), *The gender imperative: Human security vs. state security* (2nd edn.). New York and London: Routledge.

This classic collection of essays edited by feminist scholar-activists Betty Reardon and Asha Hans is now in its second edition. This is a must-read for those interested in the intersection of feminism, militarism, and human security looking at the gendered nature (and impact) of realist security discourses (and practices) of the patriarchal nation-state. By using a gendered lens to discuss security, this volume offers inspiration in rethinking alternatives to state security in factor of human security.

Reardon, B., & Snauwaert, D. (2014), *Betty A. Reardon: A pioneer in education for peace and human rights*. New York: Springer.

This book reviews and highlights the contributions of Betty Reardon to the field of peace education. The book compiles her reflections, excerpts from her seminal scholarship in the field, and covers five decades of her contributions. Divided into three generations, the authors provide essays from Betty Reardon's long career that highlight her substantive contributions and shaping of the field of peace education in distinct periods. The third generation examines contemporary thinking and reflection on the political dimensions of peace education and propositions for current and future peace educators. Reardon argues, "human rights are the ethical core of peace education" and offers several insights into alignment between the fields of critical pedagogy, Freirean education, human rights education, and peace education (147).

Ross, K. (2017), *Youth encounter programs in Israel: Pedagogy, identity and social change*. Syracuse: Syracuse University Press.

Ross carries out in-depth research of "encounter programs" that bring together Israeli Jewish and Palestinian youth in peacebuilding and dialogue efforts. The author offers a comparative perspective of two organizations in Israel—Peace Child Israel and Sadaka Reut. Ross examines how the two organizations influence participants' attitudes and identities vis-à-vis peacebuilding, citizenship, and willingness to engage with each other. The book is based on over 100 interviews with staff and former participants in the programs under study, as well as extensive observation of the organizations' activities.

Roux, C., & Becker, A. (Eds.). (2018), *Human rights literacies: Future directions*. Cham: Springer.

This book addresses concerns about the growing discordance between human rights law and human rights education, especially as realized (or not realized) materially. The first section, "Setting the Scene," criticizes the Western assumption that human rights take the form of a universal declaration, and the subsequent limitations that puts on human rights education. New literacies are introduced as a way to reframe the language used to understand human rights. The second section, "Possibilities and Probabilities," explores how a repetitive and linear "place-space-time" view of social differences—and the harmful categories of "subjects" and "failed subjects"—impacts making meaning of human rights. Contributing authors provide several studies from different areas that shed light on the different understandings of human rights within the educational context. The third section, "Unpacking Future Directions: Critiques and Conversations," argues that new epistemologies and ontologies of human rights are necessary to open up critical conversations about the future practice of human rights education.

Salomon, G., & Cairns, Ed. (Eds.). (2010), *Handbook on peace education*. New York: Taylor & Francis.

Peace education is in many ways an applied subject grounded in several different disciplines, ranging from philosophy to psychology, sociology, and political science. For that reason, Solomon and Cairns brought together researchers and academics from various disciplines to speak on peace education in practice, research on peace education, and evaluation of peace education. To best address such issues, the editors split up the volume into, first, the context of peace education, then, the contribution of underlying disciplines, and finally, approaches to peace education. The "Approaches to Peace Education" section includes chapters on promoting a culture of peace, storytelling, peace-oriented history teaching, effective program development, and more. Case studies' geopolitical contexts include Israel, Bosnia and Herzegovina, Northern Ireland, and Germany.

Salomon, G., & Nevo, B. (Eds.). (2003), *Peace education: The concept, principles, and practices around the world*. Mahwah, NJ: Lawrence Erlbaum.

Written for scholars, students, and researchers interested in peace and conflict resolution in higher education, volunteer, and public organizations, this book provides a comprehensive overview of the history of peace education, its context in relation to other academic disciplines, the main psychological and pedagogical principles of peace education, and case studies from all over the world, such as Croatia, Northern Ireland, Israel, South Africa, Rwanda, and the United States. Therefore, the book is divided into four parts: (1) concepts of peace education, (2) underlying principles of peace education, (3) case studies of peace education, and (4) research and evaluation of peace education.

Snauweart, D. (Ed.). (2019), *Exploring Betty A. Reardon's perspective on peace education: Looking back, looking forward*. New York: Springer.

This edited book pays homage to the work of pioneering peace education theorist and practitioner Betty Reardon by asking contributors: How can her foundational work be used to advance the theory and practice of peace education? Robust and nuanced, the contributors explore the impact of her work on peace and human rights education theory, pedagogy, and practice. The volume closes with a contemplative commentary by Reardon herself.

Tawil, S., & Harley, A. (Eds.). (2004), *Education, conflict, & social cohesion*. Geneva: UNESCO, International Bureau of Education.

In *Education, Conflict, and Social Cohesion*, Tawil and Harley brought together their collaborators around two central questions: (1) Are schools complicit in producing identity-based conflict? and (2) How can schools contribute to social and civic reconstruction? Throughout case studies from Bosnia-Herzegovina, Guatemala, Lebanon, Mozambique, Northern Ireland, Rwanda, and Sri Lanka, the authors weave through a common analytical framework grounded in the dynamic understandings of social cohesion as reflected in curriculum and education policy reform. In this way, the authors examined the ways in which curriculum policy is linked to national identity and citizenship. Issues such as what languages are taught in schools in a multicultural and multilingual society and contested interpretations of national history featured in curriculum are common themes throughout the various essays. Editors conclude that in order for peace education to be truly effective, researchers and educators must better understand the nuanced relationships between schooling and conflict, with particular regard to the ways in which schools shape national identity and citizenship.

Timpson, W., Brantmeier, E., Kees, N., Cavanagh, T., McGlynn, C., & Ndura-Ouédraogo, E. (2009), *147 tips for teaching peace and reconciliation*. Madison, WI: Atwood Publishing.

Written for educators, this book attempts to provide practical, usable teaching strategies for people working toward peace and reconciliation in schools and community-based contexts. "Tips" attempt to build bridges among peace educators, peace scholars, and peace activists; each tip is rooted in the theoretical and conceptual world of peace and reconciliation education. Short, pithy, and rich with personal example, the following topics and more are explored through 147 usable teaching strategies:

understanding the field of peace education; seeing the interconnections among cultural and biodiversity; understanding types and forms of conflict and restorative practices aimed at individual and communal harmony; developing emotional intelligence; building positive climates and trust; promoting creative engagement in peace and reconciliation processes; building curriculum; and understanding change for the purpose of promoting peace and reconciliation.

Verma, R. (2017), *Critical peace education & global citizenship*. New York: Routledge.

Telling the stories of teachers and learner activists, Rita Verma brings to life the potential of unofficial curricula for critical peace education. Verma does not shy away from the difficult questions that emerge when engaging with issues such as gang violence, human trafficking, oppressive gender norms, and damaging narratives of nationhood and citizenship. Data presented from classrooms with diverse populations offer instructive examples for understanding the connections between peace education and the many pressing issues affecting students and the bigger populations they exist within. *Critical Peace Education and Global Citizenship* offers an important perspective for those studying educational theory and critical pedagogy.

Zajda, J., & Ozdowski, S. (Eds.). (2017), *Globalisation, human rights education and reforms*. Dordrecht: Springer.

This book explores the (often problematic) relationship between the state and human rights education discourse in the context of recent globalization. Authors with diverse backgrounds in various fields discuss recent trends in research on globalization and HRE, as well as the pedagogy and reforms stemming from this research. Altogether, the chapters contextualize HRE discourse within global conversations around migration, nation-building, and identity politics. Thus, readers are given a thorough analysis and critique of the role of the nation-state in human rights education around the globe.

Zembylas, M., Charalambous, C., & Charalambous, P. (2016), *Peace education in a conflict-affected society: An ethnographic journey*. Cambridge: Cambridge University Press.

Peace Education in a Conflict-Affected Society is a theoretically informed ethnography of peace education policy initiatives in response to the conflict in Cyprus of the late 2000s. Though focusing on one specific case study, the authors use the Cypriot case to analyze broader theoretical and methodological frameworks. The ethnographic approach also gives particular attention to the emotional and ethical challenges that teachers face in the practice of peace education. Teacher responses to policies and practices, as well as the impacts of teacher training workshops, offer a close look at the complexities of creating and implementing initiatives in conflict-affected areas. Researchers and practitioners in the field of peace education have much to learn from the challenges and successes in Cyprus, as illuminated in this book.

Notes

Introduction

1   There are many other examples of trees being used as metaphors in education and peace studies, but we have not come across any like the "possibility" tree.

Chapter 1

1   This chapter draws from material from the previously published chapters: (1) Hantzopoulos, Zakharia and Harris-Garad (2021) and (2) Hantzopoulos and Williams (2017).
2   Since peace education happens daily and in all corners of the globe, we note here its pedagogical development as an academic field only.
3   See www.i-i-p-e.org.
4   LGBTQIA+ generally refers to lesbian, gay, bi-sexual, transgender, queer or questioning, intersex, ambiguous/ally and other non-heterosexual identified people (pansexual, gender-queer, etc.)

Chapter 2

1   This chapter draws from previously published work found in Hantzopoulos, M. (2013) The possibilities of restorative justice in US public schools: A case study of the Fairness Committee at a small NYC high school: *The Prevention Researcher*, 20(1).
2   While there are some postcolonial critiques of critical peace education (CPE), particularly in its teleological Freirean framings, definitions of CPE are explicit in their reliance on local, dynamic, fluid, and context-based approaches. Scholars like Ragland (2015, 2018), Williams (2016), Hantzopoulos (2015, 2016b), Shirazi (2011), Zakharia (2017) and Zembylas (2016, 2018) have framed CPE in this continuum.

3 Some recent examples include the Dream Defenders' efforts against police brutality, the Water Protectors fighting against the Dakota Access Pipeline, local communities in Queens resisting the corporate land-grabbing by Amazon headquarters, and so on.

4 In US schools, students of color make up more than 50 percent of the school-going population (https://nces.ed.gov/programs/coe/pdf/coe_cge.pdf), while the teaching force is 80 percent white (https://www.edweek.org/ew/articles/2017/08/15/the-nations-teaching-force-is-still-mostly.html).

5 In 2018–19, 62 percent of the students identified as Latinx, 22 percent as Black, 7 percent as white, 6 percent as Asian, and 3 percent as Other. Twenty percent receive mandated services for special education (higher than the city average of 12 percent), and approximately 80 percent qualified for free and reduced lunch, one indicator of low socioeconomic status (Inside Schools, https://insideschools.org/school/02M605).

Chapter 3

1 Some sections of this chapter draw from and expand upon previously written work, including the following chapters:
   (1) Bajaj and Mabona (2021).
   (2) Bajaj (2017).

Chapter 4

1 This chapter draws from the previously published chapter: Bajaj (2017).
2 While the requirements differ state by state in India, teachers have generally completed a multiyear teacher training course after receipt of their high school diplomas.

Chapter 5

1 This chapter draws from the previously published article and book: (1) Bajaj (2018); and (2) Hantzopoulos (2016).
2 In the United States, there has been increasing attention to the outsized influence of white families and how public schools cater to them. As an example, see the podcast "Nice White Parents" at https://www.nytimes.com/2020/07/23/podcasts/nice-white-parents-serial.html?

Chapter 6

1   These lessons have been slightly updated from the ones in Bajaj &
    Hantzopoulos (2016). Introduction. *Peace Education: International
    Perspectives*. Bloomsbury: New York.
2   The full advisory board for the Bloomsbury Academic Series on Peace &
    Human Rights Education includes the following members: Loreta Castro
    (Miriam College, Philippines), Catalina Crespo Sancho (Defensora de los
    Habitantes, Costa Rica), Nancy Flowers (Human Rights Educators-USA,
    United States), Asha Hans (formerly Utkal University, India), Andre Keet
    (Nelson Mandela University, South Africa), Margo Okazawa-Rey (formerly
    Mills College, United States), Betty Reardon (International Institute on Peace
    Education, United States), Zeena Zakharia (University of Maryland, United
    States), and Michalinos Zembylas (Open University of Cyprus, Cyprus).
3   The full questions we posed to advisory board members were as follows: (1)
    In your decades of work in the fields of peace education and human rights
    education, what, in your perspective, are the key intellectual contributions
    (concepts, frameworks, methods, analyses) that have been put forth by
    you or others? (2) What do you see as the most pressing questions that
    upcoming scholars in the field of peace and human rights education
    should be asking? (3) What advice do you have for scholars, students, and
    practitioners of peace and human rights education? (4) Given the current
    crises of our time, what types of work do you hope to see emerging from
    the fields of peace education and human rights education in the coming
    years? Not all board members were able to respond; however, we include the
    thoughts of those that were able to.
4   These questions have been slightly modified from the ones posed in
    Bajaj, M. (2015). Bajaj, M. (2015), "Pedagogies of resistance" and critical
    peace education praxis. *Journal of Peace Education, 12*(2): 154–166, and
    Hantzopoulos & Bajaj (2016). Conclusion. *Peace Education: International
    Perspectives*. Bloomsbury, New York.

Appendix

1   We are grateful for the assistance of the following students and former
    students in compiling and annotating this guide: Eunice Roh (Vassar
    College), Katherine Walters (Vassar College), and Maria Autrey (University
    of San Francisco).

References

Advancement Project, Education Law Center, FairTest, The Forum for Education and Democracy, Juvenile Law Center, & NAACP Legal Defense and Educational Fund, Inc. (2011), *Federal policy, ESEA re-authorization, and the school-to-prison pipeline*. Open Society Foundations. Retrieved from b.3cdn.net/advancement/ceb35d4874b0ffde10_ubm6baeap.pdf

Al-Daraweesh, F., & Snauwaert, D. (2015), *Human rights education beyond universalism and relativism: A relational hermeneutic for global justice*. New York: Palgrave MacMillan.

Althusser, L. (1979), *Reading capital*. London: Verso.

American Civil Liberties Union. (2010), ACLU lawsuit challenges abusive police practices in New York City schools. Retrieved from www.aclu.org/racial-justice/aclu-lawsuit-chalenges-abusive-police-practices-new-york-city-schools

Amnesty International. (2015a), *Deadly force: Police use of lethal force in the United States*, Amnesty International. https://www.amnesty.org.uk/files/webfm/Documents/issues/2015_aiusareport_deadlyforce_final.pdf?xPgkGiEfSuDt4Gz2Ksi782WPDJ5_57Y8

Amnesty International. (2015b), Human rights education. Retrieved from http://www.amnesty.org/en/human-rights-education

Ancess, J., Rogers, B., Duncan Grand, D., & Darling-Hammond, L. (2019), *Teaching the way students learn best: Lessons from Bronxdale High School*. Palo Alto, CA: Learning Policy Institute.

Annamma, S., Morrison, D., & Jackson, D. (2014), Disproportionality fills in the gaps: Connections between achievement, discipline and special education in the School-to-Prison Pipeline. *Berkeley Review of Education*, 5.

Antrop-González, R. (2011), *Schools as radical sanctuaries: Decolonizing urban education through the eyes of youth of color and their teachers*. Charlotte, NC: Information Age Pub.

Anyon, J. (1980), Social class and the hidden curriculum of work. *Journal of Education*, *162*(Winter): 67–92.

Appiah, K. A. (2005), *The ethics of identity*. Princeton, NJ: Princeton University Press.

Appiah, K. A. (2007a), *The ethics of identity*. Princeton, NJ: Princeton University Press.

Appiah, K. A. (2007b), *Cosmopolitanism: Ethics in a world of strangers*. New York: W. W. Norton & Company.

Apple, M. (1982), Reproduction and contradiction in education. In M. Apple (Ed.), *Cultural and economic reproduction in education* (pp. 1–31). London, Boston, and Henley: Routledge and Kegan Paul.

Apple, M. W., & Beane, J. A. (Eds.). (2007), *Democratic schools: Lessons in purposeful education*. Portsmouth, NH: Heinemann.

Aronowitz, S., & Giroux, H. (1993), *Education still under siege*. Westport, CT: Greenwood Publishing Group.

Bajaj, M. (2008), *The encyclopedia of peace education*. Charlotte, NC: Information Age Publishing.

Bajaj, M. (2009), 'I have big things planned for my future': The limits and possibilities of transformative agency in Zambian schools. *Compare*, *39*(4): 551–68.

Bajaj, M. (2010), Conjectures on peace education and Gandhian studies: Method, institutional development, and globalization. *Journal of Peace Education*, *7*(1): 47–63.

Bajaj, M. (2011), Human rights education: Ideology, location, and approaches. *Human Rights Quarterly*, *33*: 481–508.

Bajaj, M. (2012), *Schooling for social change: The rise and impact of human rights education in India*. New York: Bloomsbury.

Bajaj, M. (2014), The productive plasticity of rights: Globalization, education and human rights. In N. Stromquist & K. Monkman (Eds.), *Globalization and education: Integration and contestation across cultures* (pp. 51–66). Lanham, MD: Rowman and Littlefield.

Bajaj, M. (2015), 'Pedagogies of resistance' and critical peace education praxis. *Journal of Peace Education*, *12*(2): 154–66.

Bajaj, M. (2016a), In the Gaze of Gandhi: Peace education in contemporary India. In M. Bajaj & M. Hantzopoulos (Eds.), *Peace education: International perspectives* (pp. 107–22). London: Bloomsbury Publishing.

Bajaj, M. (2016b), The paradox and promise of children's rights in Indian schools. In J. Rajan & O. Dwivedi (Eds.), *Human rights and postcolonial India* (pp. 49–64). London: Routledge.

Bajaj, M. (2017a), Human rights education for social change: Experiences from South Asia. In K. Bickmore, R. Hayhoe, C. Manion, K. Mundy, & R. Read (Eds.), *Comparative and international education: Issues for teachers* (2nd edn, pp. 211–33). Toronto: Canadian Scholars Press.

Bajaj, M. (2017b), *Human rights education: Theory, research, praxis*. Philadelphia: University of Pennsylvania Press.

Bajaj, M. (2018), Conceptualizing transformative agency in education for peace, human rights & social justice. *International Journal of Human Rights Education*, *2*(1): 1–22.

Bajaj, M., Argenal, A., & Canlas, M. (2017), Socio-politically relevant pedagogy for immigrant and refugee youth. *Equity & Excellence in Education*, *50*(3): 258–74.

Bajaj, M., & Brantmeier, E. J. (2011), The politics, praxis, and possibilities of critical peace education. *Journal of Peace Education*, *8*(3): 221–4.

Bajaj, M., Canlas, M., & Argenal, A. (2017), Between rights and realities: Human rights education for immigrant and refugee youth in an urban public high school. *Anthropology and Education Quarterly*, *48*(2): 124–40.

Bajaj, M., & *Chiu, B. (2009), Education for sustainable development as peace education. *Peace & Change*, *34*(4): 441–55.

Bajaj, M., Cislaghi, B., & Mackie, G. (2016), Advancing transformative human rights education. Annex to G. Brown (Ed.), *The global citizenship commission report the universal declaration of human rights in the twenty-first century: A living document in a changing world*. Cambridge: Open Book Publishers. Retrieved from Cambridge. https://www.openbookpublishers .com/shopimages/The-UDHR-21st-C-AppendixD.pdf

Bajaj, M., & Hantzopoulos, M. (Eds.). (2016), *Peace education: International perspectives*. London: Bloomsbury Academic, an imprint of Bloomsbury Publishing, Plc.

Bajaj, M., & Mabona, N. (2021), Theories of human rights education in comparative international education: From declarations to new directions. In T. Jules, R. Shields, & M. Thomas (Eds.), *Bloomsbury handbook of theory in comparative and international education* (pp. 363–78). London: Bloomsbury.

Banks, J., & Banks, C. (1993), *Multicultural education: Issues and perspectives*. Indianapolis, IN: Wiley.

Bar-Tal, D. (2002), The elusive nature of peace education. In G. Salomon & B. Nevo (Eds.), *Peace education: The concept, principles and practice in the world*. Mahwah, NJ: Lawrence Erlbaum.

Bartlett, L. (2008), Paulo Freire and peace education. In M. Bajaj (Ed.), *Encyclopedia of peace education*. Charlotte, NC: Information Age.

Baxi, U. (1997), Human rights education: The promise of the third millenium? In G. J. Andreopoulos & R. P. Claude (Eds.), *Human rights education for the twenty-first century* (pp. 142–54). Philadelphia: University of Pennsylvania Press.

Bekerman, Z. (2016), Experimenting with integrated peace education: Critical perspectives in the Israeli context. In M. Bajaj & M. Hantzopoulos (Eds.), *Peace education: International perspectives* (pp. 51–68). London: Bloomsbury.

Bekerman, Z., & Zembylas, M. (2011), *Teaching contested narratives: Identity, memory, and reconciliation in peace education and beyond*. Cambridge: Cambridge University Press.

Bell, L. A., & Adams, M. (1997), *Teaching for diversity and social justice*. New York: Routledge.

Bellino, M. J. (2017), *Youth in postwar Guatemala: Education and civic identity in transition*. Rutgers, NJ: Rutgers University Press. Childhood Studies Series.

Bermeo, M. J. (2016a), Peace education, 3rd ed. *Journal of Peace Education*, *13*(1): 107–8.

Bermeo, M. J. (2016b), Teaching for peace in settings affected by urban violence: Reflections from Guayaquil, Ecuador. In M. Bajaj & M. Hantzopoulos (Eds.), *Peace education: International perspectives* (pp. 157–74). London: Bloomsbury Publishing.

Bickmore, K. (2011), Policies and programming for safer schools: Are 'anti-bullying' approaches impeding education for peacebuilding? *Educational Policy*, *25*(4): 648–87.

Bickmore, K. (2014), Peacebuilding (in) education: Democratic approaches to conflict in schools and classrooms. *Curriculum Inquiry*, *44*(4): 443–8.

Boal, A. (1993), *Theater of the oppressed*. New York: Theatre Communications Group.

Boccanfuso, C., & Kuhfeld, M. (2011), Multiple responses, promising results: Evidence-based, nonpunitive alternatives to zero tolerance. *Child Trends*. Available at: https://www.childtrends.org/publications/multiple-responses-promising-results-evidence-based-nonpunitive-alternatives-to-zero-tole rance [Accessed May 12, 2020].

Bourdieu, P., & Passeron, J. (1977), *Reproduction in education, society and culture*. London and Beverly Hills: Sage Publications.

Bowles, S., & Gintis, H. (1976), *Schooling in capitalist America*. London: Routledge and Kegan Paul.

BRAC. (2013), The lantern of legal literacy. In *Human Rights Education in Asia-Pacific: Volume Four* (pp. 51–60). Osaka: HuRights Osaka.

BRAC. (2014), 'Paulo Freire and Subaltern Consciousness'—a discussion by Dr. Laurence Simon. Retrieved July 28, 2015, from www.brac.net/content/'paulo-freire-and-subaltern-consciousness'-discussion-dr-laurence-simon#.Vbg JVYtQr8E

BRAC. (n.d.), BRAC Overview. Retrieved July 28, 2015, from hrls.brac.net/overview

Brantmeier, E. J. (2011), Towards mainstreaming critical peace education in US teacher education. In C. S. Malott & B. Porfilio (Eds.), *Critical pedagogy in the twenty-first century: A new generation of scholars* (pp. 349–75). Charlotte, NC: Information Age Publishing.

Brantmeier, E. J. (2013), Toward a critical peace education for sustainability. *Journal of Peace Education*, *10*(3): 242–58. doi: 10.1080/17400201.2013.862920

Brock-Utne, B. (1989), *Feminist perspectives on peace and peace education*. New York: Pergamon Press.

Bromley, P. (2014), Comparing minority and human rights discourse in social science textbooks: Cross-national patterns, 1970–2008. *Canadian Journal of Sociology, 39*(1): 1–44. doi:10.29173/cjs17001

Burke, R. (2013), *Decolonization and the evolution of international human rights*. Philadelphia: University of Pennsylvania Press.

Cardenas, S. (2005), Constructing rights? Human rights education and the state. *International Political Science Review, 26*(4): 363–79.

Chaudhary, L. (2007), An economic history of education in colonial India. Retrieved July 28, 2015, from economics.ucr.edu/seminars_colloquia/2007/political_economy_development/LatikaChaudhary5-6-07.pdf

Chavez, K., & Griffin, C. (2009), Power, feminisms, and coalitional agency: Inviting and enacting difficult dialogues. *Women's Studies in Communication, 32*(1): 1–11.

Christle, C. A., Jolivette, K., & Nelson, C. M. (2005), Breaking the school to prison pipeline: Identifying school risk and protective factors for youth delinquency. *Exceptionality, 13*(2): 69–88.

Christle, C. A., Jolivette, K., & Nelson, C. M. (2007), School characteristics related to highschool dropout rates. *Remedial and Special Education, 28*: 325–39.

Chubbuck, S. M., & Zembylas, M. (2011), Toward a critical pedagogy for nonviolence in urban school contexts. *Journal of Peace Education, 8*(3): 259–75.

Cislaghi, B., Gillespie, D., & Mackie, G. (2017), Expanding the aspirational map: Interactive learning and human rights in Tostan's community empowerment program. In M. Bajaj (Ed.), *Human rights education: Theory, research and praxis* (pp. 251–68). Philadelphia: University of Pennsylvania Press.

Clark, N. (2013), Indian study abroad trends: Past, present and future. Retrieved July 28, 2015, from wenr.wes.org/2013/12/indian-study-abroad-trends-past-present-and-future/

Community Asset Development Redefining Education (CADRE). (2010), Redefining parenting in South LA Schools. *guidestar.org*. Available at: https://www.guidestar.org/profile/26-4753821 [Accessed May 12, 2020].

Coysh, J. (2017), *Human rights education and the politics of knowledge*. London: Routledge.

Crenshaw, K. W., Ocen, P., & Nanda, J., *Black girls matter: Pushed out, overpoliced, and underprotected* (pp. 1–53). Report. Center for Intersectionality and Social Policy Studies, Columbia University and African American Policy Forum.

Danesh, H. B. (2006), Towards an integrative theory of peace education. *Journal of Peace Education, 3*(1): 55–78.

Darder, A. (2014), *Freire and education*. New York: Routledge.

Davidson, J. (2014), Restorative justice. *Education Digest, 80*(3): 19.

De Certeau, M. (1984), *The practice of everyday life*. Berkeley: University of California Press.

De Jesús, A. (2012), Authentic caring and community driven reform: The case of El Puente Academy for Peace and Justice. In M. Hantzopoulos & A. Tyner-Mullings (Eds.), *Critical small schools: Beyond Privatization in New York City urban educational reform* (pp. 63–78). Charlotte, NC: Information Age.

de los Reyes, E., & Patricia G. (2001), *Pockets of hope: How students and teachers change the world*. Westport, CT: Bergin and Garvey.

Del Felice, C., Karako, A., & Wisler, A. (Eds.). (2015), *Peace education evaluation: Learning from experience and exploring prospects*. Charlotte, NC: Information Age Publishing.

Dewey, J. (1916), *Democracy and education*. New York: MacMillan.

Diaz Soto, L. (2005, Fall–Winter), How can we teach peace when we are so outraged? A call for critical peace education. *Taboo: The Journal of Culture and Education, 9*(2): 91–6.

Dierker, B. (2016), 'You Are Building on Something': Exploring agency and belonging among African American young adults. In J. DeJaeghere (Ed.), *Education and youth agency: Advancing responsible adolescent development* (pp. 27–46). New York: Springer.

Dietrich, W. (2012), Transrational interpretations of peace. *Interpretations of Peace in History and Culture*, 210–69. doi: 10.1057/9780230367715_6.

Dietrich, W. (2013), *Elicitive conflict transformation and the transrational shift in peace politics*. Basingstoke, Hampshire: Palgrave Macmillan.

Dietrich, W. (2018), *Elicitive conflict mapping*. London: Palgrave Macmillan UK.

Douzinas, C. (2007), *Human rights and empire: The political philosophy of cosmopolitanism*. New York: Routledge.

Duckworth, C. (2008), Maria Montessori and peace education. In M. Bajaj (Ed.), *Encyclopedia of peace education* (pp. 33–8). Charlotte, NC: Information Age Publishing.

Duckworth, C. (2015), *9/11 and collective memory in US classrooms: Teaching about terror*. New York: Routledge.

Dunlevy, E. (2014), Negotiating competing ethical systems in schools: Restorative practices for transforming violent school communities. *Journal of Peace Education and Social Justice, 8*(1): 57–61.

Düwell, M., Braarvig, J., Brownsword, R., & Mieth, D. (Eds.). (2014), *The Cambridge handbook of human dignity: Interdisciplinary perspectives*. Cambridge: Cambridge University Press. doi:10.1017/CBO9780511979033

Echavarría Alvarez, J., Ingruber, D., & Koppensteiner, N. (Eds.). (2018), *Transnational Resonances: Echoes to the many peaces*. Cham: Palgrave MacMillan.

Eden, M. (2017), School discipline reform and disorder: Evidence from New York City public schools, 2012–16. *The Education Digest*, 83(1): 22.

Epstein, R., Blake, J., & González, T. (2017), *Girlhood interrupted: The erasure of Black girls' childhood*. Georgetown University Law Center on Poverty and Inequality.

Evans, S. (2002), Macaulay's minute revisited: Colonial language policy in nineteenth-century India. *Journal of Multilingual and Multicultural Development*, 23(4): 260–81.

Fenning, P., & Rose, J. (2007), Overrepresentation of African American students in exclusionary discipline the role of school policy. *Urban Education*, 42(6): 536–59.

Fergusen, A. (2001), *Bad boys: Public schools in the making of black masculinity*. Ann Arbor: University of Michigan Press.

Flowers, N. (2003), What is human rights education? In *A survey of human rights education*. Retrieved from http://www.hrea.org/erc/Library/curriculum_methodology/flowers03.pdf

Foley, D. (1991), Rethinking school ethnographies of colonial settings: A performance Perspective of reproduction and resistance. *Comparative Education Review*, 35(3): 532–51.

Foster, K. (2015), 'Pushed out of School for Being Me': New York City's struggle to include youth and community voices in school discipline reform. *Voices in Urban Education*, 42: 43–9.

Freire, P. (1970/2000), *Pedagogy of the oppressed*. New York: Bloomsbury Academic.

Galtung, J. (1969), Violence, peace, and peace research. *Journal of Peace Research*, 6(3): 167–91.

Galtung, J. (1976), Three approaches to peace: Peacekeeping, peacemaking, and peacebuilding. In *Peace, war, and defense: Essays in peace research* (Vol. 2). Prio Monographs, Issue 5. Copenhagen: Christian Ejlers.

Gay, G. (1994), *A synthesis of scholarship in multicultural education*. Washington, DC: Office of Educational Research and Improvement.

Gilmore, R. W. (2007), *Golden gulag: Prisons, surplus, crisis, and opposition in globalizing california*. Berkeley: University of California Press.

Giroux, H. (1996), *Fugitive cultures: Race, violence, and youth*. New York: Routledge.

Giroux, H. (1997), *Pedagogy and the politics of hope*. Boulder, CO: Westview Press.

Grant, C. (1977), *Multicultural education: Commitments, issues and applications*. Washington, DC: Association for Supervision and Curriculum Development.

Grant, C., & Sleeter, C. (1986), Race, class, and gender in educational research: An argument for integrative analysis. *Review of Educational Research, 56*: 195–211.

Gregory, A., Soffer, R., Gaines, E., Hurley, A., & Karikehalli, N. (2016), Implementing restorative justice in schools: Lessons learned from restorative justice practitioners in four Brooklyn schools. *Brooklyn Community Foundation*. Available at: https://www.brooklyncommunityf oundation.org/sites/default/files/lessons_learned_about_early_implemen tation_of_restorative_justice_in_schools_for_distribution.pdf [Accessed July 1, 2020].

Gur-Ze'ev, I. (2001), Philosophy of peace education in a post-modern era. *Educational Theory, 51*: 315–36.

Hantzopoulos, M. (2010), Encountering peace: The politics of participation when educating for co-existence. In P. P. Trifonas & B. Wright (Eds.), *Critical Issues in Peace and Education* (pp. 21–39). New York: Routledge.

Hantzopoulos, M. (2011a), Deepening democracy: How one school's Fairness Committee offers an alternative to 'discipline'. *Rethinking Schools* in *Schools: Studies in Education, 8*(1): 112–16.

Hantzopoulos, M. (2011b), Institutionalizing critical peace education in public schools: A case for comprehensive implementation. *Journal of Peace Education, 8*(3): 225–42.

Hantzopoulos, M. (2012a), When cultures collide: Students' successes and challenges as transformative change agents within and beyond a democratic school. In M. Hantzopoulos & A. Tyner-Mullings (Eds.), *Critical small schools: Moving beyond privatization in New York City public school reform* (pp. 189–212). Charlotte, NC: Information Age Publishing.

Hantzopoulos, M. (2012b), Human rights education as public school reform. *Peace Review: A Journal of Social Justice, 24*: 36–45.

Hantzopoulos, M. (2013), The possibilities of restorative justice in US public schools: A case study of the fairness committee at a small NYC high school. *The Prevention Researcher, 20*(1): 7–10.

Hantzopoulos, M. (2015), Sites of liberation or sites of despair?: The challenges and possibilities of democratic education in an urban public school in New York City. *Anthropology and Education Quarterly, 46*(4): 345–62.

Hantzopoulos, M. (2016a), *Restoring dignity in public schools: Human Rights Education in Action*. New York: Teachers College Press.

Hantzopoulos, M. (2016b), Beyond American exceptionalism: Centering critical peace education in US school reform. In M. Bajaj & M. Hantzopoulos (Eds.), *Peace education: international perspectives* (pp. 177–92). New York: Bloomsbury.

Hantzopoulos, M., & Bajaj, M. (2016), Conclusion: Critical directions for peace education. In M. Bajaj & M. Hantzopoulos (Eds.), *Peace education: International perspectives* (pp. 233–8). London: Bloomsbury.

Hantzopoulos, M., & Williams, H. (2017), Peace education as a field. In M. Peters (Ed.), *Encyclopedia of educational philosophy and theory*. Singapore: Springer.

Hantzopoulos, M., Zakharia, Z., & Harris-Garad, B. (2021), Peace theories. In T. Jules, R. Shields, & M. Thomas (Eds.), *Bloomsbury handbook of theory in comparative and international education* (pp. 347–62). New York: Bloomsbury.

Harris, I. M. (2004), Peace education theory. *Journal of Peace Education, 1*(1): 5–20.

Harris, I. M. (2008), History of peace education. In M. Bajaj (Ed.), *Encyclopedia of peace education*. Charlotte, NC: Information Age Publishing.

Harris, I. M., & Morrison, M. L. (2003), *Peace education*. Jefferson, NC: McFarland & Company.

Hayhoe, R., Manion, C., & Mundy, K. (2017), Why study Comparative Education? In K. Bickmore, R. Hayhoe, C. Manion, K. Mundy, & R. Read (Eds.), *Comparative and international education: Issues for teachers, second edition* (pp. 2–26). Toronto: Canadian Scholars' Press.

Hicks, D. (1988), *Education for peace: Issues, principles, and practice in the classroom*. Abingdon: Routledge.

Holland, T., & Martin, J. P. (2017), Human rights education's role in peacebuilding: Lessons from the field. In M. Bajaj (Ed.), *Human rights education: Theory, research, and praxis* (pp. 267–90). Philadelphia: University of Pennsylvania Press.

Honwana, A. (2002), Negotiating postwar identities: Child soldiers in Mozambique and Angola. In N. Gibson & G. Bond (Eds.), *Contested terrains and constructed categories: Contemporary Africa in focus* (pp. 277–98). Boulder: Westview Press.

hooks, b. (1994), *Teaching to transgress: Education as the practice of freedom*. New York: Routledge.

Howlett, C. (2008), John Dewey and peace education. In M. Bajaj (Ed.), *Encyclopedia of peace education*. Charlotte, NC: Information Age.

HRW. (2015), *Marry before your house is swept away: Child marriage in Bangladesh*. New York: Human Rights Watch.

Humanities Preparatory Academy, Restorative Justice and Fairness. *Humanities Preparatory Academy*. Available at: https://humanitiesprep.org/restorative-justice-and-fariness [Accessed May 12, 2020].

'Inside Schools, Humanities Preparatory Academy'. *InsideSchools*. Available at: https://insideschools.org/school/02M605 [Accessed May 12, 2020].

Islam, A., Khan, A., Chodhuary, S., & Samadder, M. (2012), *Exploring legal aid services of BRAC HRLS programme in Cox's Bazar*. Dhaka: BRAC.

Jeffrey, C. (2012), Geographies of children and youth II: Global youth agency. *Progress in Human Geography, 36*(2): 245–53.

Jenkins, T. (2008), International Institute on Peace Education (IIPE) & Community-Based Institutes on Peace Education (CIPE). In M. Bajaj (Ed.), *Encyclopedia of peace education*. Online resource. Accessed at: https://www .tc.columbia.edu/epe/epe-entries/Jenkins_IIPE_28feb08.pdf

Jensen, E. (2015), *School-based youth courts: Student perceptions of school climate, safety, and disciplinary measures*. New York: Center for Court Innovation.

Jocson, K. M. (2007), *Youth media matters: Participatory cultures and literacies in education*. Minneapolis: University of Minnesota Press.

Kabeer, N. (2002), *The power to choose: Bangladeshi women and labour market decisions in London*. London: Verso.

Kadam, K. N. (1991), *Dr. Babasaheb Ambedkar and the significance of his movement: A chronology*. Bombay: Popular Prakashan.

Kapoor, D. (2004), Popular education and social movements in India: State responses to constructive resistance for social justice. *Convergence, 37*(2): 55–63.

Katz, S., & Spero, A. M. (Eds.). (2015), *Bringing human rights education to US classrooms: Exemplary models from elementary grades to university*. New York: Palgrave.

Keet, A. (2007), *Human rights education or human rights in education: A conceptual analysis*. (PhD dissertation), University of Pretoria.

Keet, A. (2010), A conceptual typology of human rights education and associated pedagogical forms. *Journal of Human Rights Education, 1*(1): 30–41.

Keet, A. (2017), Does human rights education exist?, *International Journal of Human Rights Education, 1*(1): 1–18.

Keet, A. (2018), Criticism and critique: Critical theory and the renewal of citizenship, democracy and human rights education. In M. Zembylas & A. Keet (Eds.), *Critical human rights, citizenship, and democracy education: Entanglements and regenerations* (pp. 17–34). London: Bloomsbury.

Kennelly, J. J. (2009), Youth cultures, activism and agency: Revisiting feminist debates. *Gender and Education, 21*(3): 259–72.

Kester, K., & Cremin H. (2017), Peace education and peace education research: Toward a concept of poststructural violence and second-order reflexivity. *Educational Philosophy and Theory, 49*(14): 1415–27.

Khoja-Moolji, S. (2014), Producing neoliberal citizens: Critical reflections on human rights education in Pakistan. *Gender and Education, 26*(2): 103–18. doi: 10.1080/09540253.2014.898025

Klevan, S. L. (2018), *Understanding restorative approaches to discipline through the lens of authority: A case study of a New York City high school* (Unpublished dissertation). Available from ProQuest Dissertation and Master's Theses database. UMI No. 10931305.

Klevan, S. L., & Villavicencio, A. (2016), Strategies for improving school culture: Educator reflections on transforming the high school experience for Black and Latino young men. Executive summary. *Research Alliance for New York City Schools*.

Klocker, N. (2007), An example of 'Thin' agency: Child domestic workers in Tanzania. In R. Panelli, S. Punch, & E. Robson (Eds.), *Global perspectives on rural childhood and youth* (pp. 83–94). New York: Routledge.

Koenig, S. (1997), Foreword. In G. J. Andreopoulos & R. P. Claude (Eds.), *Human rights education for the twenty-first century* (pp. xiii–xvii). Philadelphia: University of Pennsylvania Press.

Kolisetty, A. (2014), *Examining the effectiveness of legal empowerment as a pathway out of poverty: A case study of BRAC justice & development working paper series*. Washington, DC: World Bank.

Krücken, G., & Drori, G. S. (Eds.). (2010), *World society: The writings of John W. Meyer*. Oxford: Oxford University Press.

Krueger, P. (2010), It's not just a method! The epistemic and political work of young peoples' lifeworlds at the school–prison nexus. *Race Ethnicity and Education*, *13*(3): 383–408.

Kurian, N. (2020), 'Kindness isn't important, we need to be scared': disruptions to the praxis of peace education in an Indian school. *Journal of Peace Education*. doi: 10.1080/17400201.2020.1728237

Kwon, S. A. (2013), *Uncivil youth: Race, activism and affirmative governmentality*. Durham, NC: Duke University Press.

Ladson-Billings, G., & Henry, A. (1980), Blurring the borders: Voices of African liberatory pedagogy in the United States and Canada. *Journal of Education*, *172*(2): 72–88.

Lee, T., Cornell, D., Gregory, A., & Fan, X. (2011), High suspension schools and dropout rates for Black and White students. *Education & Treatment of Children*, *34*(2): 167–92.

Legewie, J., Farley, C., & Stewart, K. (2019), *Aggressive policing and academic outcomes: Examining the impact of police "Surges" in NYC*. The Research Alliance for New York City Schools.

Levinson, B. A., Foley, D. E., & Holland, D. C. (1996), *The cultural production of the educated person: Critical ethnographies of schooling and local practice*. New York: SUNY Press.

Levinson, B. A., Gross, J. P. K.Hanks, C., Dadds, J. H., Kumasi, K., & Link, J. (2011), *Beyond critique: Exploring critical social theories and education*. New York: Routledge.

Lewis, S. (2009), *Improving school climate: Findings from schools implementing restorative practices*. Bethlehem, PA: International Institute for Restorative Practices.

Lin, J., Oxford, R., & Brantmeier, E. J. (Eds.). (2013), *Re-envisioning higher education: Embodied paths to wisdom and social transformation*. Charlotte, NC: Information Age Publishing.

Lustick, H. (2017), What are we restoring?. In N. S. Okilwa, M. Khalifa, & F. M. Briscoe (Eds.), *Black teachers on restorative discipline', The school to prison pipeline: The role of culture and discipline in school (Advances in Race and Ethnicity in Education, Volume 4)* (pp. 113–34). Bingley: Emerald Publishing Limited.

MacLeod, J. (1995), *Ain't no making it*. Boulder, CO: Westview Press.

Magendzo, A. (1994), Tensions and dilemmas about education in human rights in democracy. *Journal of Moral Education, 23*(3): 251–9.

Magendzo, A. (1997), Problems in planning human rights education for reemerging latin American democracies. In R. P. Claude & G. Andreopoulos (Eds.), *Human rights education for the twenty first century* (pp. 469–83). Philadelphia: University of Pennsylvania Press.

Magendzo, A. K. (2005), Pedagogy of human rights education: A Latin American perspective. *Intercultural Education, 16*(2): 137–43.

Manassah, T., Roderick, T., & Gregory, A. (2018), A promising path toward equity. *The Learning Professional, 39*(4): 36–40.

Marsh, V. L. (2017), *Becoming restorative: Three schools transitioning to a restorative practices culture*. Rochester: Center for Urban Education Success.

Mayfield, J. B. (2012), *Field of reeds: Social, economic and political change in Rural Egypt: In search of civil society and good governance*. Bloomington, IN: AuthorHouse.

Mazama, A., & Lundy, G. F. (2012), African American homeschooling as racial protectionism by Ama Mazama and Garvey Lundy. *Journal of Black Studies, 43*(7) (October): 723–48.

McGinn, N. (1996), Education, democratization, and globalization: A challenge for comparative education. *Comparative Education Review, 40*(4): 341–57.

McGlynn, C. (2009), Negotiating cultural differences in divided societies: An analysis of approaches to integrated education in Northern Ireland. In C. McGlynn, M. Zembylas, Z. Bekerman, & T. Gallagher (Eds.), *Peace education in conflict and post-conflict societies: Comparative perspectives* (pp. 9–25). New York: Palgrave MacMillan.

McGlynn, C., Zembylas, M., Bekerman, Z., & Gallagher, T. (Eds.). (2009), *Peace education in conflict and post-conflict societies: Comparative perspectives*. New York: Palgrave MacMillan.

McLaren, P. (1996), Liberatory politics and higher education: A Freirean perspective. In H. A. Giroux, C. Lankshear, M. Peters, & P. McLaren (Eds.), *Counternarratives: Cultural studies and critical pedagogies in postmodern spaces* (pp. 117–48). New York: Routledge.

Meiners, E. R., & Winn, M. T. (2010), Resisting the school-to-prison pipeline: The practice to build abolition democracies. *Race, Ethnicity, and Education*, *13*(3): 271–6.

Meintjes, G. (1997), Human rights education as empowerment: Reflections on pedagogy. In G. Andreopoulos & R. P. Claude (Eds.), *Human rights education for the twenty first century* (pp. 64–79). Philadelphia: University of Pennsylvania Press.

Mejias, S. (2017), Politics, power, and protest: Rights-based education policy and the limits of human rights education. In M. Bajaj (Ed.), *Human rights education: Theory, research, and praxis* (pp. 170–94). Philadelphia: University of Pennsylvania Press.

Merry, S. (2006), *Human rights and gender violence: Translating international law into local justice*. Chicago: University of Chicago Press.

Meyer, J. W., Bromley-Martin, P., & Ramirez, F. O. (2010), Human rights in social science textbooks: Cross-national analyses, 1970–2008. *Sociology of Education*, *83*(2): 111–34.

Mignolo, W. (2000), *Local histories/global designs: Coloniality, subaltern knowledge, and border thinking*. Princeton, NJ: Princeton University Press.

Mignolo, W. (2018), Foreword on pluriversality and multipolarity. In B. Reiter (Ed.), *Constructing the pluriverse: The geopolitics of knowledge* (pp. ix–xvi). Durham, NC: Duke University Press.

Ministry of Foreign Affairs, Government of the Bahamas. (2016), Ministry of Foreign Affairs and Immigration Issues Travel Advisory for Bahamians traveling to United States of America. *Ministry of Foreign Affairs - Bahamas*. Available at: https://mofa.gov.bs/ministry-of-foreign-affairs-and-immigrat ion-issues-travel-advisory-for-bahamians-traveling-to-united-states-of -america/ [Accessed May 12, 2020].

Miron, L., & Lauria, M. (1998), Student voice as agency: Resistance and accommodation in inner-city schools. *Anthropology & Education Quarterly*, *29*(2): 189–213.

Monahan, R. (2010, February 4), Queens girl Alexa Gonzalez hauled out of school handcuffed after getting caught doodling on desk. *Newsday*. Retrieved from www.newsdaynews.com

Montessori, M. (1949), *Education and peace*. (H. R. Lane, Trans). Chicago, IL: Henry Regenry.

Morris, E. W. (2005), 'Tuck in that Shirt!' Race, class, gender, and discipline in an urban school. *Sociological Perspectives*, *48*(1): 25–48.

Morris, M. W. (2016), *Pushout: The criminalization of Black girls in schools*. New York: The New Press.

Morris, E. W., & Perry, B. L. (2016), The punishment gap: School suspension and racial disparities in achievement. *Social Problems*, *63*(1): 68–86.

Morsink, J. (1999), *The universal declaration of human rights: Origins, drafting, and intent*. Philadelphia: University of Pennsylvania Press.

Murithi, T. (2009), An African perspective on peace education: Ubuntu lessons in reconciliation. *International Review of Education*, 55(2–3): 221–33.

Murphy, K., Sean, P., & Dylan, W. (2016), The opportunities and limitations of educational interventions in countries with identity-based conflicts. In M. Bajaj and M. Hantzopoulos (Eds.), *Peace Education: International Perspectives* (pp. 35–50). London and New York: Bloomsbury.

Murphy-Graham, E. (2009), Constructing a new vision: Undoing gender through secondary education in Honduras. *International Review of Education*, 55(5–6): 503–21.

Nakagawa, M., & Wotipka, C. M. (2016), The worldwide incorporation of women and women's rights discourse in social science textbooks, 1970–2008. *Comparative Education Review*, 60(3): 501–29.

Naseem, M. A., & Arshad-Ayaz, A. (2017), Creating 'Invited' spaces for counter-radicalization and counter-extremism education. *Diaspora, Indigenous, and Minority Education*, 11(1): 6–16.

National World War II Museum. (n.d.), Research starters: Worldwide deaths in World War II. Retrieved from https://www.nationalww2museum.org/studen ts-teachers/student-resources/research-starters/research-starters-worldwide -deaths-world-war

New York Civil Liberties Union, Make the Road, & Annenberg Institute of School Reform (2009), *Safety with dignity: Alternatives to the over-policing of schools*. New York: New York Civil Liberties Union.

Nieto, S., & Bode, P. (1992), *Affirming diversity: The sociopolitical context of multicultural education*. Boston: Pearson.

Noguera, P. (2003), *City schools and the American dream: Reclaiming the promise of public education*. New York: Teachers College Press.

Noguera, P., Cammarota, J., & Ginwright, S. (2006), *Beyond resistance! Youth activism and community change: New democratic possibilities for practice and policy for America's youth*. New York: Routledge.

Noguera, P., & Cannella, C. (2006), Youth agency, resistance, and civic activism: The public commitment to social justice. In P. Noguera, J. Cammarota, & S. Ginwright (Eds.), *Beyond resistance: Youth activism and community change* (pp. 333–47). New York: Routledge.

Novelli, M., & Smith A. (2011), *The role of education in peacebuilding: A synthesis report of the findings from Lebanon, Nepal, and Sierra Leone*. New York: UNICEF.

O'Connor, C. (1997), Disposition towards (collective) struggle and educational resilience in the inner city: A case of six African-American high school students. *American Educational Research Journal*, 34(4): 593–629.

Ogilvie, G., & Fuller, D. (2016), Restorative justice pedagogy in the ESL classroom: Creating a caring environment to support refugee students. *TESL Canada Journal, 33*(10): 86–96. https://doi.org/10.18806/tesl.v33i0.1247

Osler, A., & Starkey, H. (2010), *Teachers and human rights education.* Stoke: Trentham Books.

Padilla, M. (2019), Officer under investigation after arresting 6-year-olds, chief says. *The New York Times.* Available at: https://www.nytimes.com/2019/09 /22/us/6-year-old-arrested-orlando-florida.html [Accessed May 12, 2020].

Paris, D., & Alim, S. (2017), *Culturally sustaining pedagogies: Teaching and learning for justice in a changing world.* New York: Teachers College Press.

Peiser, J. (2020, September 8), A Black seventh-grader played with a toy gun during a virtual class. His school called the police. Washington Post. Available at: https://www.washingtonpost.com/nation/2020/09/08/black-student-suspended-police-toy-gun/

Picower, B. (2012), *Practice what you teach: Social justice education in the classroom and the streets.* New York: Routledge.

Ragland, D. (2015), Betty Reardon's philosophy of peace education and the centrality of justice. *Journal of Peace Education, 12*(1): 37–55.

Ragland, D. (2018), Radical truth telling from the Ferguson Uprising: An educational intervention to shift the narrative, build political efficacy, claim power, and transform communities. In H. Shapiro (Ed.), *The Wiley handbook on violence in education: Forms, factors, and preventions* (pp. 519–36). Hoboken, NJ: Wiley-Blackwell.

Ramirez, F., Suarez, D., & Meyer, J. (2007), The worldwide rise of human rights education. In A. Benavot, C. Braslavsky, & N. Truong (Eds.), *School knowledge in comparative and historical perspective* (pp. 35–52). Netherlands: Springer.

Rana, P., & Sugden, J. (2013), India's record since independence. Retrieved July 28, 2015, from blogs.wsj.com/indiarealtime/2013/08/15/indias-record-since -independence/

Reardon, B. (1985), *Sexism and the war system.* New York: Teachers College Press.

Reardon, B. (1988), *Comprehensive peace education: Educating for social responsibility.* New York: Teachers College Press.

Reardon, B. (1996), *Sexism and the war system.* Syracuse: Syracuse University Press.

Reardon, B. (2000), Peace education: A review and projection. In B. Moon, S. Brown, & M. Ben Peretz (Eds.), *International companion to education* (pp. 397–425). New York: Routledge.

Reardon, B. (2001), *Education for a culture of peace from a gendered perspective.* Paris: UNESCO.

Reay, D. (2004), 'It's all becoming habitus': Beyond the habitual use of habitus in educational research. *British Journal of Sociology of Education*, 25(4): 431–44.

Rivera-McCutchen, R. (2012), Considering context: Exploring a small schools' struggle to maintain its educational vision. In M. Hantzopoulos & A. Tyler-Mullings (Eds.), *Critical Small Schools: Beyond privatization in New York City urban educational reform* (pp. 21–39). Charlotte, NC: Information Age.

Robinson, T., & Ward, J. (1991), 'A belief in self far greater than anyone's disbelief': Cultivating resistance among African American female adolescents. In C. Gilligan, A. Rogers, & D. Tolman (Eds.), *Women, girls and psychotherapy: Reframing resistance* (pp. 87–103). New York: Haworth.

Rodriguez, L., & Conchas, G. (2008), *Small schools and urban youth: Using the power of school culture to engage students*. Thousand Oaks, CA: Sage.

Romano & Ragland (2018), Truth-telling from the margins: Exploring Black-led responses to police violence and systemic humiliation. In D. Rothbart (Ed.), *Systemic humiliation in America* (pp. 145–72). Cham: Palgrave Macmillan.

Ross, K. (2017), *Youth encounter programs in Israel*. Syracuse, NY: Syracuse University Press.

Rumberger, R. W. (2004), Why Students drop our of school? In G. Orfied (ed.). *Dropouts in America: Confronting the graduation rate crisis* (pp. 131–55). Cambridge, MA: Harvard University Press.

Russell, G., & Suarez, D. (2017), Symbol and substance: Human rights education as an Emergent Global Institution. In M. Bajaj (Ed.), *Human rights education: Theory, research and praxis* (pp. 19–46). Philadelphia: University of Pennsylvania Press.

Russell, S. G., Sirota, S. L., & Ahmed, A. K. (2019), Human rights education in South Africa: Ideological shifts and curricular reforms. *Comparative Education Review*, 63(1):1–27.

Sandwick, T., Hahn, J. W., & Ayoub, L. H. (2019), Fostering community, sharing power: Lessons for building restorative justice school cultures. *Education Policy Analysis Archives*, 27: 145.

Shah, P. P. (2016), Agency as negotiation: Social norms, girls' schooling and marriage in Gujarat, India. In J. DeJaeghere (Ed.), *Education and youth agency: Advancing responsible adolescent development* (pp. 85–102). New York: Springer.

Shah, R., Maber, E., Lopes Cardozo, M., & Paterson, R. (2016), *UNICEF programme report (2012–2016): Peacebuilding, education and advocacy in conflict-affected contexts programme*. New York: UNICEF.

Shirazi, R. (2011), When projects of 'empowerment' don't liberate: Locating agency in a 'postcolonial' peace education. *Journal of Peace Education*, 8(3): 277–94.

Skiba, R. J., Arredondo, M. I., & Williams, N. T. (2014), More than a metaphor: The contribution of exclusionary discipline to a school-to-prison pipeline. *Equity & Excellence in Education*, *47*(4): 546–64.

Smillie, I. (2009), *Freedom from want: The remarkable success story of BRAC, the global grassroots organization that's winning the fight against poverty.* Boulder, CO: Kumarian Press.

Smith, A., McCandless, E., Paulson, J., & Wheaton, W. (2011), *The role of education in peacebuilding: Literature review.* New York: UNICEF.

Snauwaert, D. (2008), The moral and spiritual foundations of peace education. In M. Bajaj (Ed.), *Encyclopedia of peace education.* Charlotte, NC: Information Age Publishing.

Solorzano, D., & Bernal, D. D. (2001), Examining transformational resistance through a crtiical race and LatCrit theory framework: Chicano and Chicana students in an urban context. *Urban Education*, *36*(3): 308–42.

Spreen, C. A., & Monaghan, C. (2017), Leveraging diversity to become a global citizen: Lessons for human rights education. In M. Bajaj (Ed.), *Human rights education: Theory, research, praxis* (pp. 291–316). Philadelphia: University of Pennsylvania Press.

Steinborn, M. L., & Nusbaum, E. A. (2019), Cripping human rights education with disability studies: An undergraduate reading list. *Educational Studies*, *55*(4): 489–504. doi:10.1080/00131946.2019.1630128

Suarez, D. (2007), Education professionals and the construction of human rights education. *Comparative Education Review*, *51*(1): 48–70.

Suh, S., & Suh, J. (2007), Risk factors and levels of risk for high school dropouts. *Professional School Counseling*, *10*: 297–306.

Sullivan, E. (2007), *Deprived of dignity: Degrading treatment and abusive discipline in New York City and Los Angeles public schools.* New York: National Economic and Social Rights Initiative.

Sumida Huaman, E. (2011), Transforming education, transforming society: The co-construction of critical peace education and Indigenous education. *Journal of Peace Education*, *8*(3): 243–58.

Sumida Huaman, E. (2017), Indigenous Rights Education (IRE): Indigenous knowledge systems and transformative human rights in the Peruvian Andes. *International Journal of Human Rights Education*, *1*(1): 1–34.

Synott, J. (2005), Peace education as an educational paradigm: Review of a changing field using an old measure. *Journal of Peace Education*, *2*(1): 3–16.

Tandon, Y. (1989), Peace education: Its concepts and problems and its application to Africa. In *Militarism and peace education in Africa* (pp. 50–76). Nairobi: African Association for Literacy and Adult Education.

Tarrow, N. (1992), Human rights education: Alternative conceptions. In J. Lynch, C. Modgil, & S. Modgil (Eds.), *Human rights, education and global responsibilities* (pp. 21–50). London: Falmer Press.

'The Hindu' Editorial. (2012), India loses 3 million girls in infanticide. Retrieved July 28, 2015, from www.thehindu.com/news/national/india-loses -3-million-girls-in-infanticide/article3981575.ece

Tibbitts, F. (2001), Prospects for civics education in transitional democracies: Results of an impact study in Romanian classrooms. *Intercultural Education*, *12*(1): 27–40.

Tibbitts, F. (2002), Understanding what we do: Emerging models for human rights education. *International Review of Education*, *48*(3–4): 159–71.

Tibbitts, F. (2005), Transformative learning and human rights education: Taking a closer look. *Intercultural Education*, *16*(2): 107–13.

Tibbitts, F. (2008), Human rights education. In M. Bajaj (Ed.), *Encyclopedia of peace education* (pp. 99–108). Charlotte, NC: Information Age Publishing.

Tibbitts, F. (2017), Evolution of human rights education models. In M. Bajaj (Ed.), *Human rights education: Theory, research, praxis* (pp. 69–95). Philadelphia: University of Pennsylvania Press.

Tjersland, H., & Facci, P. D. (2019), Introduction: Unfolding transrational potential. *Journal of Peace Education*, *16*(3): 247–51. doi: 10.1080/17400201.2019.1697070

Toh, S. H. (2006), Education for sustainable development and the weaving of a culture of peace: Complementarities and synergies. Paper presented at the UNESCO Expert Meeting on Education for Sustainable Development. Available at: http://citeseerx.ist.psu.edu/viewdoc/download?doi=10.1.1.493 .1182&rep=rep1&type=pdf

Tostan. (n.d.), Tostan: Dignity for all. Retrieved from https://www.tostan.org/

Truthtellingproject.org https://ttppoliceviolence.businesscatalyst.com/

Tsolakis, M. (2013), Citizenship and transformative human rights education: Surveys as 'Praxis' in the São Paulo periphery. *Journal of Social Science Education*, *12*(3): 39–50.

Tuck, E. (2009), Re-visioning action: Participatory action research and Indigenous theories of change. *The Urban Review*, *41*(1): 47–65.

Tuck, E. (2012), *Urban youth and school pushout: Gateways, get-aways, and the GED*. London: Routledge.

Tutu, D. (1999), *No future without forgiveness*. New York: Penguin.

Tyner-Mullings, A. (2015), *Enter the alternative school: Critical answers to questions in urban education*. Boulder, CO: Paradigm Publishers.

UNICEF. (2018), *An everyday lesson: #ENDviolence in schools*. New York: UNICEF.

UNICEF. (2020), Bangladesh-statistics. Retrieved July 28, 2020, from www.u nicef.org/infobycountry/bangladesh_bangladesh_statistics.html

United Nations. (1948), *Universal declaration of human rights*. New York.

United Nations. (1993), *Vienna declaration*. Vienna.

United Nations. (1998), Retrieved from guidelines for national plans of action for human rights education. https://www.ohchr.org/EN/Issues/Education/Training/Compilation/Pages/GuidelinesforNationalPlansofActionforHumanRightsEducation(1997).aspx

Vincent, C. G., Sprague, J. R., & Tobin, T. J. (2012), Exclusionary discipline practices across students racial/ethnic backgrounds and disability status: Findings from the pacific northwest. *Education and Treatment of Children*, *35*(4): 585–601.

Wadhwa, A. (2015), *Restorative justice in urban schools: Disrupting the school-to-prison pipeline*. London: Routledge.

Wahl, R. (2014), Policing, values, and violence: Human rights education with law enforcers in India. *Oxford Journal of Human Rights Practice*, *5*(2): 220–42.

Wahl, R. (2016), Learning world culture or changing it? Human rights education and the police in India. *Comparative Education Review*, *60*(2): 293–319.

Wahl, R. (2017), *Just violence: Torture and human rights in the eyes of the police*. Stanford, CA: Stanford University Press.

Weis, L. (1996), Forward. In B. A. Levinson, D. E. Foley, & D. C. Holland (Eds.), *The cultural production of the educated person: Critical ethnographies of the educated person*. New York: SUNY Press.

Welch, K., & Payne, A. (2011), Exclusionary school punishment. *Youth Violence and Juvenile Justice*, *10*(2): 155–71.

West, C. (2004), *Democracy matters: Winning the fight against imperialism*. New York: Penguin.

White, S. C., & Choudhury, S. A. (2007), The politics of child participation in international development: The dilemma of agency. *The European Journal of Development Research*, *19*(4): 529–50.

Williams, H. M. A. (2013), Postcolonial structural violence: A study of school violence in Trinidad and Tobago. *International Journal of Peace Studies*, *18*(2): 39–64.

Williams, H. M. A. (2016), Lingering colonialities as blockades to peace education: School violence in Trinidad. In M. Bajaj & M. Hantzopoulos (Eds.), *Peace education: International perspectives* (pp. 141–56). London: Bloomsbury Publishing.

Williams, H. M. A. (2017), Teachers' nascent praxes of care: Potentially decolonizing approaches to school violence in Trinidad. *Journal of Peace Education*, *14*(1): 69–91.

Williams, H. M. A., & Bermeo, M. J. (2020), A decolonial imperative: pluriversal rights education. *International Journal of Human Rights Education*, *4*(1): 1–33.

Willis, P. (1977), *Learning to labour: How working class kids get working class jobs*. New York: Columbia University Press.

Wilson, M. A. F., Yull, D. G., & Massey, S. G. (2020), Race and the politics of educational exclusion: explaining the persistence of disproportionate disciplinary practices in an urban school district. *Race Ethnicity and Education*, 23(1): 134–57.

World Bank. (2014), Addressing inequality in South Asia: Policy reforms as important as economic growth. Retrieved July 28, 2015, from www.worldb ank.org/en/news/feature/2014/12/04/addressing-inequality-policy-reforms -important-economic-growth

World Bank. (2015), Bangladesh data. Retrieved July 28, 2015, from data .worldbank.org/country/bangladesh

Wynter, S. (1994, Fall), No humans involved: An open letter to my colleagues. *Forum H.H.I. Knowledge for the 21st Century*, 1(1): 42–73.

Wynter, S. (2003), Unsettling the coloniality of being/power/truth/freedom: Towards the human, after Man, its overrepresentation—An argument. *CR: The New Centennial Review*, 3(3): 257–337.

Yang, W. (2015), Afterword: Will human rights education be decolonizing?. In S. Katz & A. M. Spero (Eds.), *Bringing human rights education to US classrooms: Exemplary models from elementary grades to university* (pp. 225–35). New York: Palgrave

Zakharia, Z. (2016), Peace education and peacebuilding across the conflict continuum: Insights from Lebanon. In M. Bajaj & M. Hantzopoulos (Eds.), *Peace education: International perspectives* (pp. 71–88). New York: Bloomsbury.

Zakharia, Z. (2017), Getting to 'no': Locating critical peace education within resistance and anti-oppression pedagogy at a Shi'a Islamic school in Lebanon. *Research in Comparative & International Education*, 12(1): 46–63.

Zakharia, Z., & Bishop, L. M. (2013), Towards positive peace through bilingual community education: Language efforts of Arabic speaking communities in New York. In O. García, Z. Zakharia, & B. Otcu (Eds.), *Bilingual community education and multilingualism: Beyond heritage languages in a global city* (pp. 169–89). Bristol: Multilingual Matters.

Zembylas, M. (2011), Peace and human rights education: Dilemmas of compatibility and prospects for moving forward. *Prospects*, 41(4): 567–79. doi: 10.1007/s11125-011-9212-8

Zembylas, M. (2016), Emotions, trauma and critical pedagogy: Implications for critical peace education. In M. Bajaj & M. Hantzopoulos (Eds.), *Peace Education: International Perspectives* (pp. 19–33). London: Bloomsbury Academic.

Zembylas, M. (2017), Re-contextualising human rights education: Some decolonial strategies and pedagogical/curricular possibilities. *Pedagogy, Culture & Society*, 25(4): 487–99. doi:10.1080/14681366.2017.1281834

Zembylas, M. (2018), Con-/divergences between postcolonial and critical peace education: Towards pedagogies of decolonization in peace education. *Journal of Peace Education, 15*(1): 1–23.

Zembylas, M. (2020), Toward a decolonial ethics in human rghts and peace education. *International Journal of Human Rights Education, 4*(1): 1–21.

Zembylas, M., & Bekerman, Z. (2013), Peace education in the present: Dismantling and reconstructing some fundamental theoretical premises. *Journal of Peace Education, 10*(2): 197–214.

Index

acceptance 46, 53–4
activism 15, 63, 70, 71, 74, 109, 129,
        132, 141, 144, 145
    intergenerational 109
Addams, Jane 18
Afghanistan 79–80, 89
African American 36, 105, 110
agency 28, 42–3, 49–50, 58, 64, 67, 76,
        87, 92–3, 96, 99, 104–14, 134
    coalitional 71, 109–10, 121
    collective 42, 107
    community 40
    localized 35
    relational 108–9
    strategic 111
    sustained 107–8
    transformative 2, 7, 28, 72, 93,
        95–9, 105, 108–13, 115, 126
Amnesty International 40, 54–5, 58,
        63, 73

Bangladesh 77, 79, 81, 83–4, 88–93,
        109
Boal, Augusto 66, 69
BRAC 81, 83–4, 89–93
Brock-Utne, Birgit 21

Chile 52, 66–7, 82, 141
citizenship 56, 59, 71, 74–5, 93, 99,
        132, 135, 138, 142, 145, 146, 147,
        149, 150
    active 54–5
    global 7, 21, 23, 59–60, 72, 96, 129,
        137, 150
Civil Rights 19
civil society 1, 17

coexist 113, 117
coexistence 59, 130
Cold War 19, 53, 144
Combahee River Collective 124
conflict 21, 31–2, 38, 59, 67–8, 103,
        111, 117, 118, 120–1, 123–4,
        129–35, 138–40, 144, 147–51
    class 17
    direct 19
    post 68, 103, 129–33, 140, 148
    resolution 25, 133, 140, 143, 148
    zones 31, 38
conscientization 23, 59, 92, *see also*
        critical consciousness
cosmopolitanism 31, 59–60, 110, 145
Council of Europe 118
counternarratives 40, 117
critical consciousness 2, 6, 7, 60,
        63–4, 70, 72, 82–3, 93, 96, 99,
        102, 104–5, 109–10, *see also*
        conscientization
critical pedagogy 28, 67, 102, 104, 133,
        134, 143, 147, 150
Cyprus 76, 119, 125, 130, 151, 154

declarationist 59, 76
decolonial 11–12, 15–16, 24, 27–8, 32,
        37, 49, 59, 60, 64, 70, 75–7, 97,
        101, 113, 115, 120–1, 125
democracy 18, 22, 46–7, 56, 66–8, 71,
        75, 86, 102, 120, 135, 142, 145
    democratic participation 49
development 11–12, 15–21, 38, 45,
        53–4, 56–8, 66, 80, 86, 89–91, 95,
        108, 118–19, 131–2, 137–8, 140,
        148, 152

Dewey, John   18, 22, 24, 82, 99

dialogical   2, 39, 42, 63, 66, 71, 102
  nondialogical   130

dialogue   6, 32, 41, 46–8, 64, 66, 69, 86,
  96, 108–9, 116, 125, 143, 147

dignity   18–20, 25, 42–3, 50, 51, 54,
  68, 71, 80, 92–3, 95–6, 98–104,
  112–14, 115, 125–6, 136, 138

disability   76–7

education   17–21, 51–7, 61, 79–84,
  95–9
  characteristic   23, 63, 68, 69, 76, 106
  coexistence   59, 113, 117, 130
  critical peace   27–31, 35–6, 38, 42,
    71, 97, 115, 119, 120, 121, 134,
    150, 152, 154
  culturally relevant   89
  early childhood   56
  emancipatory   106
  girls   69, 79–80, 82, 88, 90, 107–9
  global peace   27
  history   133–4
  human rights (*see* human rights
    education (HRE))
  liberatory   6, 95–102, 104, 106, 112,
    114, 116
  multicultural   25, 101, 131, 149
  non-formal   12–13, 32, 51, 55, 60–1,
    66, 68–9, 73, 82, 84, 88, 89–90, 98,
    102, 126, 127
  peace (*see* peace, education)
  popular   2, 55, 66–8, 83, 90
  values   23, 28, 41, 47–9, 54, 58, 109,
    133–4, 145, 146

emotion   31, 45, 56, 76, 130, 138, 150–1

empathy   24, 41, 96, 103, 121, 132, 144

empowerment   23, 59–60, 64, 92, 106,
  132
  community   68, 82, 89, 133
  legal   81
  women's   89

enforcement   40, 52

engagement   2–3, 13, 37, 44, 58, 72, 81,
  96, 99, 100, 106, 113, 121, 123,
  125, 145, 146, 150

equity   7, 16, 51, 96
  inequity   20, 42

Eurocentric   11, 76, 77, 113, 116

Europe   17–18, 27, 72, 75, 79, 104, 116,
  118, 129

experiential learning   22–3

feminism   146
  Black feminist   124
  feminist   21, 108, 110, 118–19,
    121–5, 146

First World War (WWI), *see* World War
  I

Freire, Paulo   2, 10, 13, 23–4, 59–60,
  62–4, 66, 70, 82–3, 92–3, 99, 104–
  5, 107, 110, 116, 118, 147, 152

future   2, 13, 16, 28, 33, 36–7, 51, 53,
  68, 77, 91, 93, 99, 105, 111, 113,
  117, 121, 125, 129, 132, 137,
  147–8
  agentic   112
  alternative   37
  liberatory   39
  sustainable   2, 13, 21, 25, 37

Galtung, Johan   20, 29, 62, 137

Gandhi, Mohandas   19, 82, 93, 99, 131,
  144

Gandhian studies   19

gender   33, 54, 86–7, 91, 92, 106, 110,
  119, 120, 122, 124, 139, 146, 152
  discrimination   86, 100
  equality   68, 122, 133
  identity   7, 139
  inequity   108, 119
  lens   21
  norms   109, 134, 150
  stereotype   91
  violence   32, 70, 93

genocide   53, 57

girls   44, 69, 79–80, 82, 88, 90, 107–9
global citizenship   7, 21, 23, 59–60, 72,
        96, 129, 137, 150
globalization   57, 93, 135, 141, 150
Global South   19, 38, 80–1, 109, 118,
        122

Honduras   108
Humanities Preparatory
        Academy   46–8, 71, 138
human rights   1, 6–7, 10, 12, 18, 20,
        40, 42, 52–60, 66–4, 67–70,
        72–7, 79–81, 83, 85–8, 90–3,
        96–7, 100–101, 103, 110–11,
        113, 119–20, 122, 123, 127, 129,
        132, 133, 134, 136, 137, 139, 142,
        144–8
    abuse   87, 137
    framework   62, 77, 80–1, 100, 138,
        145
    Human Rights Day   53
    Human Rights Friendly Schools
        (HRFS)   54, 63, 73
    international   53, 58, 62, 80, 100,
        132, 138, 145
    law   89–93, 133, 137
    violations   89–90, 103
human rights education (HRE)   1–2,
        6–7, 10–13, 25, 50, 51–77, 79–81,
        83–93, 95–8, 100–104, 108, 110,
        112–29, 133–6, 138, 140–5,
        147–50, 154
    community-based   11, 13, 36, 55,
        58, 63, 66, 70, 81, 93, 143
    critical   77, 81, 83, 95, 98, 100, 115,
        119–21, 134, 142, 147
    decolonial   59, 75–6, 96–7, 101, 113,
        115, 120–1
    explicit   36, 61, 70, 71, 73, 84
    history   51–3, 116
    Human Rights Education
        Review   61
    implicit   36, 61, 71, 73

Institute for Human Rights Education
        (IHRE)   70, 81, 85–8, 128
institutionalization   52, 55, 60, 62,
        126
International Journal of Human
        Rights Education   61
K–12, 69–74, 81, 84–5, 124, 141
non-formal   55, 66, 69, 73, 90, 118,
        127
policy   53, 60, 62, 64, 67, 69–70, 81,
        84, 92, 129, 134, 135, 137, 146
school-based   12–13, 55, 70, 77, 79,
        84, 89–90, 93, 102–3, 112, 118,
        124, 138, 141, 143, 145
textbook   55, 62, 64, 69–70, 77, 81,
        83, 85–7
transformative   12, 24, 42, 59–61,
        69–73, 77, 81, 83–4, 87, 92–3,
        97–8, 115, 120–1, 126, 129
identity   130, 147, 149, 150
    collective   110
    gender   139
India   19, 52, 63, 70, 74, 77, 79–89,
        92–3, 107–10, 118, 128–9, 133–4,
        139, 141, 143, 153, 154
indigenous rights education   64, 76
injustice   6, 12, 20, 38–9, 41–2, 54, 71,
        80–1, 86, 89, 91, 99, 109–10, 112,
        120
Institute of Human Rights
        Education   86, 128
integrated schooling   31
integrated schools   130
intergenerational   39–40, 76, 109, 125
interventions   29, 87

justice   1, 6–10, 12, 16, 18, 20, 33, 35,
        39, 42–3, 47, 55, 56, 66, 71, 73, 84,
        88, 91–3, 96, 102, 107, 110, 126,
        132, 136, 139, 140, 141, 142
    community   15
    dialogical   39
    educational   25

global   127
racial   38, 41–2
restorative   35–6, 39, 41, 42, 46,
    48–9, 152
social (*see* social justice)
transformative   12, 36, 40

Latin America   17, 55, 66–7, 72, 116,
    118, 129
Lesbian, Gay, Bisexual, Transgender,
    Intersex, Queer (LGBTIQ)   33,
    152

Mayan   24, 110
media   44, 99
    literacy   132
    social   125
memory   130
    collective   67, 130, 135
Mexico   68, 139
methods   2, 23, 54, 70, 83, 86, 93, 102,
    135, 154
micropolitics   65
migrant   72, 125
Millennium Development Goals
    (MDGs)   80
Montessori, Maria   18, 22–4, 99

neo-colonial   19, 29, 121
neoliberalism   62
Nobel Peace Prize   18, 24, 80
non-governmental organizations
    (NGOs)   12, 15, 55, 57, 60, 68,
    70, 73, 80–1, 84, 88, 89, 129, 133,
    134

organization   18, 27, 41, 52, 63, 81–6,
    89
    community-based   70, 107

Pakistan   74, 79–80, 89, 134
participatory   55, 61, 66–9, 86–7, 90–1,
    99, 102, 116, 121

methods   54, 102
pedagogies   12, 72, 81
research   2–3
peace   1–2, 6–7, 10–12, 16–31, 33,
    37–8, 47, 53, 54, 57, 80, 96, 101,
    108, 113, 118–23, 125–6, 128,
    130–3, 135–7, 139–46, 149
    activist   139, 144, 149
    building   1, 15, 22, 68, 101, 122, 140,
        142, 147
    education   1, 6–7, 10–13, 15–19,
        21, 23–33, 35–52, 55, 60, 62, 71,
        83, 93, 95–8, 100–104, 108, 112,
        115–20, 123, 125–6, 128–37,
        139–54
    making   24, 124, 131
    negative   16, 20–1, 37, 96
    positive   7, 16, 19, 20–1, 25, 37, 45,
        96, 143
    studies   16–18, 20–1, 27, 31, 118,
        140, 152
pedagogy   2, 10, 16, 21–4, 27, 63, 65,
    66, 69, 82, 86, 92, 98, 102, 107,
    113, 119, 128, 131, 136, 138, 139,
    140, 143, 146, 147, 149, 150
    critical   28, 87, 102, 104, 133, 134,
        143, 147, 150
    Freirean   2, 82
    participatory   12, 72, 81
People's Watch   12, 81, 83–5, 87, 93
Philippines   89, 118, 133, 139, 154
plural   16, 111
    pluralism   86
possibility tree   1, 2, 6, 8, 10, 96–7, 152
postcolonial   28, 31, 35, 37–9, 62, 64,
    74, 120, 125, 152
post-structural   2, 15, 27–8, 31, 37, 64
power   3, 12, 21, 28, 37, 59, 62–4, 72,
    81, 99, 106–7, 109, 111, 121, 125,
    128, 130, 134, 135
praxis   2, 29, 36, 49, 63, 64, 76, 96, 99,
    100–103, 107, 110, 114, 116, 120,
    121, 123, 126, 129, 132, 142, 154

problem tree   2–3, 6, 10
Project Melel   68

racism   20–1, 28, 35–9,
      41, 56–7
    antiracism   96
    structural   29, 39, 42
    systemic   36
Reardon, Betty   21, 27, 37, 100, 103,
      118, 132, 146, 147, 149, 154
reconciliation   24, 31, 40–1, 55, 67, 76,
      130, 131, 134, 149, 150
refugee   72, 125
resistance   39–40, 64–5, 74, 76, 82,
      104–6, 121, 132, 154
    transformational   105
rights   18, 20, 25, 51–2, 55, 56, 58–63,
      69–74, 76, 79–80, 84, 86, 89–93,
      100–103, 110, 116, 118–19, 121,
      125, 133, 136, 138
    children's   68, 85–6
    Civil Rights Movement   19
    collective   52, 101
    cultural   52
    disability   76–7
    equal   12, 55, 81, 101
    Indigenous   76
    individual   62, 77
    legal   57
    students'   79, 86

Satyarthi, Kailash   80
scholarship   1, 11–13, 15, 25, 30–1, 38,
      51–2, 61, 63, 66, 69, 73, 75, 106–7,
      124, 147
    educational   27, 29, 30, 37, 64
    feminist   21, 110
    future   13
    global   51, 63, 77
    Indigenous   32
Second World War (WWII), see World
      War II
settler-colonial   19, 35, 38, 49

social change   7, 12, 42, 58, 60, 70–1,
      74, 82, 89, 98, 101, 104, 105, 109,
      118, 128, 146, 147
social justice   13, 21, 30, 54, 73, 76,
      108–9, 118, 128, 136, 140–3, 145
    education   95–8, 102, 104, 106, 109,
      111, 113–14, 128
social movements   52, 55, 70, 81, 86,
      101, 118
solidarity   41, 60, 64, 71, 75–6, 96, 99,
      103, 109, 110, 121, 124, 145
South Africa   19, 24, 69, 130, 148, 154
South Sudan   89
struggle   40, 50, 105–6, 110, 118, 139,
      141
Sustainable Development Goals
      (SDGs)   80

Tanzania   76, 107, 134
teachers   12, 18, 23, 29–30, 45–9, 55,
      56, 60, 67, 70–1, 73, 76, 82, 85–8,
      90, 93, 102, 108, 117, 124, 129–33,
      138, 139, 145, 150, 151
    agency   104
    Teacher's College   26–7, 138, 145
    training   81, 85–7, 153
Theater of the Oppressed   66, 69
tolerance   43, 45–6, 53, 54, 131, 134,
      136, 137, 138, 144, 146
torture   16, 57, 67, 74
Tostan   68–9, 133
transformative learning   104
trauma   39–40, 67, 98, 135
Truth and Reconciliation Commission
      (South Africa)   24
Truth Telling Project (TTP)   12, 36,
      39–42, 43, 49
Tutu, Desmond   24

ubuntu   24, 96, 110
Uganda   89, 139
UNESCO   27, 56, 149
UNICEF   56

United Nations   1, 18, 27, 51–4, 57, 85,
    100–101, 119, 124, 133, 142
United Nations Declaration on Human
    Rights Education and Training
    (UNDHRET)   53, 145
United States   12, 19, 35–50, 52, 71, 75,
    103, 106, 115, 133, 135, 138–41,
    144, 145, 148, 153, 154
    exceptionalism   38
Universal Declaration of Human Rights
    (UDHR)   18, 51–3, 56, 80,
    100–101, 133
    Article 26   52–3, 80

values   23, 28, 41, 47–9, 54, 58, 109,
    133, 134, 145, 146
vernacular   79
violence   1, 10, 15–21, 28–32, 37–51,
    53, 62, 98, 103, 107, 110–11, 113,
    116–17, 119, 120, 125, 136, 139,
    145, 150
    behavioral   20
    cultural   18, 20, 29–30, 36–8, 49
    daily   109, 110
    direct   7, 16, 20, 36, 39, 42, 133, 145
    discursive   29
    gender   70, 86, 93

indirect   42
nonviolence   18–19, 21, 23, 25, 27,
    29, 144
physical   20, 38
police   7, 12, 35, 39–42
political   20
racial   12, 35, 39–40
school   29–30, 131, 137–8
state-sanctioned   32, 36, 39–42
structural   16, 20–1, 24–5, 29–30,
    35–8, 40, 51, 109, 133
youth   25, 68, 86
Virginia   72

West Africa   68
women   33, 40, 68, 74, 77, 81–4, 88–93,
    108, 118–20, 122, 123, 125, 134,
    145
Women Leaders of Tomorrow (WLT)   74
World War I (WWI)   18
World War II (WWII)   17–18, 51–2

Yousafzai, Malala   80
youth   3, 25, 29, 31, 36, 43–5, 77, 79, 89,
    93, 105–7, 110–11, 113, 125, 138,
    144, 147
    marginalized   103